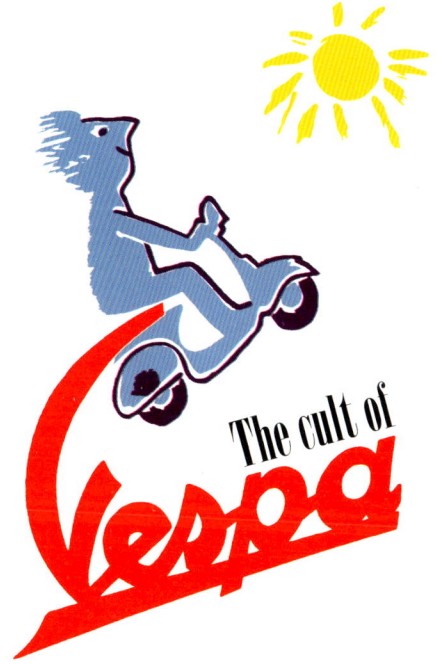

The cult of

Edited by
Omar Calabrese

Texts by
Umberto Eco
Omar Calabrese
Maurizio Bettini
Tommaso Fanfani
François Burkhardt
Francesca Picchi
Sebastiano Vassalli
Francesco Alberoni
Marino Livolsi
Gilberto Filippetti
Alessandro Baricco
Antonio Tabucchi
Lina Wertmuller

Lupetti

The cult of Vespa

PIAGGIO

Piaggio
External Relations and Communication
Viale Rinaldo Piaggio, 23
56025 Pontedera (Pisa)
Tel. +39.587.272111

Graphic design
Andrea Rauch
Layout
Silvia Pacchiarini
Cover by
Raymond Savignac

Realisation and print
Lupetti - Editori di Comunicazione S.r.l.
Via Hayez, 12
20129 Milano
Tel. +39.2.202025 Fax 20404340
www.lupetti.com

Translation by
Ron Packham
Geoff J. Phillips

Distribuited by
Gingko Press GmbH
Hamburger Strasse 180
22083 Hamburg - *Germany*
Tel. 040-291425 Fax 040-291055

Gingko Press Inc.
5768 Paradise Drive
Suite J
Corte Madera, CA 94925 - *USA*
tel. 415-9249615 Fax 415-9249608

Contents

A cult object

The first edition of the book "The **Vespa** Legend" was published in 1996 to mark the **Vespa**'s 50th birthday.

Few products reach the milestone of fifty years in production. But the **Vespa**'s extraordinary story is amazing if we remember how and when the formula was first born: in post second world war Italy, the company relaunched and literally reinvented itself by creating two-wheeled mass motorisation, thanks to the intuition of Enrico Piaggio and Corradino D'Ascanio.

Vespa, a utility vehicle whose lines were dictated exclusively by parameters such as function and cost, became an international commercial success, a leading player in the history of costume and cinema, a cult object that has sparked off associations and inspired collectors the world over.

Above all, the **Vespa** is still alive in the imagination of numerous generations, and is one of the best - known Italian trademarks and words wherever you go.

The authors of this book, with their stories and analyses covering a wide range of aspects - architecture, semiotics, anthropology, sociology, economic history - help us to understand how the **Vespa** "legend" was born and why it continues to survive.

All the articles in this book share one constant element: a fondness for the **Vespa**. The same fondness is displayed by customers and the public, anywhere in the world that people talk about this Italian product, so recognisable and famous, born way back in 1946 and still an extremely modern instrument of individual mobility.

The Piaggio Group now has a heritage that has few equals in the world, at least in the two-wheeled vehicle sector. It is a great opportunity, but an equally great responsibility. Brands such as **Vespa**, Gilera and Piaggio demand the design and development of products worthy of their names.

We think we have met this implicit expectation. With the new **Vespa** generation, which also made its entry on the U.S. market at the end of 2000, the most difficult operation was undertaken: to renew the legend, not only the styling but also attention to the customer's needs and to society's needs. Elegant design, comfort, safety and maximum environmental compatibility all blend together in a vehicle that is now enjoying the great popularity of all **Vespa** models.

Accompanied by the numerous photographs collected and catalogued in the Piaggio Historical Archives, this book also bears witness to the sense of responsibility that our company feels with relation to its historical heritage, the best example of which is the Piaggio - Giovanni Alberto Agnelli Museum now housed in the oldest part of the company's Pontedera plant.

Preserving the memory of the past, a few steps from the laboratories in which the vehicles of the future are designed, is a way of paying homage to our history, to our company and to all the people who, by their work and genius, have helped to nurture and spread its image around the world. Homage also to over a century of technological progress, which coincides with the growth of the company and Italian presence in the world.

Dante Razzano
Piaggio Group Chairman

F. Mosca

The forbidden Vespa-fruit

Umberto Eco

As I take up my pen to respond to the invitation to write something about what undoubtedly was, and has continued to be, a social phenomenon of post-war Italy, I hesitate, because I realise that this is a phenomenon which passed me by at a certain distance. I went zig-zagging through the joyful parade of **Vespas** on my antique bike like an outsider, albeit not wholly indifferent. Now that I am called upon to bear witness to this phenomenon, I realise that the truth is not so much that the **Vespa** didn't concern me, but that I removed its presence from my mind because, for me, it was like a forbidden fruit.

To put it in what is by now a dated terminology, it was a question of both economic structure and ideology. I belonged to a family which was undoubtedly not rich, but not poor, either. An office-worker's family, whose pride lay in the fact that the children had everything they needed, in the way of food, clothes, education, and a month's holiday in the countryside every year, renting a couple of rooms from distant relations who were farmers.

This comfortable situation was only possible thanks to thrifty administration, a horror for waste, and a calm indifference to the superfluous. Perhaps I should remind my readers of the economic conditions of Italian families immediately before and after the Second World War, when every middle-class family dreamt, as a famous Italian song says, of having "one thousand liras a month".

I remember that one day, shortly before the war, my father came home, had dinner with us in silence, as if something were troubling him, and then, almost secretively, as he was washing his hands in the bathroom with the door ajar, shyly called my mother and said to her, "By the way, 'the Lawyer' has given me a present of one thousand liras". 'The Lawyer' was the owner of the firm my father worked for (in Piemonte, not only Agnelli, but anybody with a degree in law - which at the time meant practically every graduate - was a lawyer). I don't know whether my father's monthly salary had already reached one thousand liras, but the sum was undoubtedly (as we used to say) an unexpected "windfall", an extraordinarily generous gift *una tantum*, which was a token of esteem and satisfaction (and was therefore primarily a source of moral gratification); and, as we shall see, rather than offering a remedy for a situation of poverty, the wealth brought by this gift of one thousand liras opened the way to the dizzy heights of "something extra" for my family.

My mother answered excitedly, "Oh, then we can buy a radio!"

Thus the radio entered into my home: it was a large Telefunken with an alarming kind of design, a mixture of the towers of Mongo (the planet of Ming where Flash Gordon had landed) and the flimsy brownish skyscrapers of *Blade Runner*. The *dernier cri* of a technology that was considered to be beyond all possible improvement, with a mobile, flickering eye for the tuning. I would spend hours, not only listening to the national programmes, but building up a Hertzian geography of my own, tracking down exotic gurgles on the green, red and yellow illuminated panel, which proffered the names of mysterious stations that could only be picked up on the short-wave bands: Riga, Tallin, Hilversum.

But I haven't been invited to write about the radio. You can imagine, though, that in that post-war period, as we were gradually getting used to the delights of white bread again (it didn't happen immediately; it took a few years), the appearance of the **Vespa** was like an event in a world that existed near mine, but didn't concern me directly, on the same level as Dakotas, or jeeps, or a Hammond organ. The thought would never have crossed my mind that I could ask my father for a scooter, as I continued to pedal around on my pre-war bike, with its tyres all patched up as a result of dozens of tiring repair jobs. My request would have aroused such amazement that it never occurred to me that I could make it. Consequently, I didn't even feel the need for this unthinkable possession.

And yet the **Vespas** were there, racing past me, all around me, ridden by boys of my age, or a little older. And this is the point where ideology comes in.

I was a member of a Catholic youth group, which made a distinction between those who lived for an ideal and those who took life as a diversion. On the one side, us, who sacrificed our Sundays in serious meetings, organising sports teams, or theatrical groups, and on the other side, the others, who on Sundays went dancing or - a symbol of the ritual consumption of wealth (highly envied, I must confess) - skiing. And every day, at a certain time, the others (who included many boys I went to school with, and even some close friends of mine) entered into another world. In that other world, They had their **Vespas**. For me, the **Vespa** went together with the *boogie woogie* and the snow-capped Alpine peaks.

They would jump on it at the gates of the school, where we had been united by the same fears and the same schoolboy tricks up to a few minutes before. In the evening, they would arrive on their **Vespas** in the square where we whiled away hours chattering on the benches, opposite a fountain that was usually not working, and some of them would tell stories they had heard about brothels, or revues with Wanda Osiris - and those who had heard these stories acquired a kind of morbid fascination in the eyes of the rest.

Thus the **Vespa** came to be linked in my eyes with transgression, sin, and even temptation - not the temptation to possess the object, but the subtle seduction of faraway places where the **Vespa** was the only means of transport. And it entered into my imagination not as an object of desire, but as a symbol of an unfulfilled desire.

I fell in love, as sometimes happens at that age. I used to write poems about my languidly Platonic love stories in secret, because it seemed impossible to declare my passion openly to the unattainable She, the lovely flower beside which I felt like an importunate worm. At the end of lessons, I think the boys used to leave school first. And so I used to go along the road with my friends in the opposite direction to my house, and then say goodbye to them after five minutes, and turn back with the busy air of one who is going home for lunch, knowing that on the way I would meet Her, in the gay company of her girl-friends (another sign of the times: the two sexes used to go home without dividing up into couples).

I would meet the group of girls, and look at my Beloved, and my day was made; I was in seventh heaven!

But sometimes the girl was not together with the group, and as I hurried on, fearing that some jealous divinity had stolen her from me, something terrible happened, something much less sacral, or - if sacral - infernal. She was still there, in front of the school steps, as if waiting for someone. And up drove (on a **Vespa**) a boy that I couldn't compete with, because he was already an undergraduate, tall, fair-haired, disdainful (and he nonchalantly told his friends that a plaster that he wore on his neck for a few days was to cover up a syphiloma).

He helped her on to the **Vespa**, and each time, the perverse pillion-rider - so much the more desirable - escaped from my clutches forever.

But worse followed; it was the period when the scandalously short, almost knee-length skirts of the war years (due, I believe, more to a lack of material than to a desire to seduce) and the bell-bottomed knee-length ones that graced the fiancées of Rip Kirby in the first

American comics that returned to the newspaper kiosks, were being substituted by long, flowing skirts that came half-way down the calf. Probably the younger generations of to-day, who have been deprived of any erotic shock by the sporting nonchalance of the mini-skirt and hot pants, cannot imagine what perverse grace, what airy elegance a long skirt gave to a girl, as she clung to her driver on the back seat of a **Vespa** that swept away, and then disappeared.

It was like the fluttering of an oriflamme, a coy floating in the wind that held innumerable suggestions of ostentatious reticence (if the oxymoron gets the idea across), a hymn of glory to femininity through the interposed symbol; the **Vespa** sailed regally away leaving in its wake a singing foam, and the sporting of mystical dolphins. And then nothing was left.

This is what the **Vespa** was for me. A magical instrument, which I never really desired, because it was beyond every possible desire, and at the same time, it frustrated my desire - or rather, it made it sublime, allowing it to live in an incorruptible world - and perhaps it was just as well: nothing is lovelier in my memory than the suffering of those vain passions.

Fifty years of industrial mythology
Omar Calabrese

Piaggio is one of the best-known and best-loved Italian firms around the world. Most of the merit for this is obviously due to its main product, the **Vespa**, which has sold millions and millions of scooters since 1946, becoming a stable part of contemporary life. But the success of the **Vespa** cannot be understood without bearing in mind the fact that it received a significant contribution from a particular kind of industrial "philosophy", surprisingly *avant-garde* in the field of Italian manufacturing industries. This "philosophy" consists of the ability with which the group has succeeded in presenting the image of the most famous scooter in the world, connecting it closely with the myths and the trends of the society into which it was introduced. The **Vespa** was not just a simple industrial product, but also a "communications workshop". Let us consider, then, its fundamental course of development.

The large-scale strategies

The first element that turned the **Vespa** into such a great success on the sales level, and therefore also on the level of ideas, lies in the anomaly of its invention: the **Vespa** is the result of a multiplicity of ideas. The idea of the low wheels joined together by a frame comes from aeronautics, and roughly corresponds to the landing gear. Motoring offered the idea of turning the frame into a body, causing the engine and the tank to disappear from view, and reducing the noise. Motorcycling supplied the concept of a driving seat uniting the typical motor-bike seat with that of the sidecar, which was so popular during the war. The novelty of the product was thus guaranteed, but together with a few references to something familiar "already seen", which makes it acceptable to everyone.

The second fundamental strategy is the one which leads the prospective customer to consider the **Vespa** as useful. The policy of mass motorisation, which was developed by Piaggio as well as others, appealed above all to the working class, who were not very rich, and who found in the scooter the initial response to their growing needs of consumption. They found this above all in its selling price and its maintenance costs, which were accessible even for the less fortunate. The target customer in this period was basically the head of the family, who might be an office clerk or a factory worker. And together with him, all the rest of the family participated in the consumption, especially if they were still young, but mature. Unlike the moped, the **Vespa** gives an impression of safety, can put up with a minimum of bad weather, doesn't get you dirty like vehicles with an open engine, and can therefore transport the basic nucleus of the family, that is to say, the couple. What's more, women have a role in the image of the use of the **Vespa**: the comfortable pillion seat, the lower position, and the absence of any wheels with spokes make it possible to adopt a travelling position that does not give rise to scandal, and is formally unexceptionable. Furthermore, the **Vespa** has a broad seat, and even a child can be transported with a certain degree of tranquillity.

Another fundamental strategy, however, is that of pleasure. The **Vespa** was offered to the post-war public in Italy as an object of their imagination and an exercise of their desire. And it is true that during the 40's and the 50's, it was a true object of mass pleasure. It was the ideal accompaniment, for example, for the first popular holidays after the War. It is probably not by chance that the image of the **Vespa** as a means of locomotion for tourists was born just a few miles away from Versilia, where it was distributed in a capillary manner right from the beginning. The **Vespa** was born as a simple, economical, comfortable, poor vehicle; but with the awareness of its being an attractive object, original though not unique, and of transmitting mythical sensations.

The strategies that have been outlined, however, are implemented in the **Vespa** and its communications apparatus in various ways, which we will now try to examine more in greater detail, analysing the object in itself, in its function as a message, its primary customers, who, in turn, are capable in their consumption of involuntarily producing further messages regarding **Vespa** and on behalf of **Vespa**, and its secondary customers, that is to say, those who do not possess a **Vespa**, or those who never will.

The industrial product

The basic reason for the myth of the **Vespa** obviously lies in the conditions amid which it was born in the post-war period. The company had suffered the destruction of various parts of its factories, and was forced to adapt its wartime production to the new period of peace. And Enrico Piaggio had the idea which turned out to be a winner. The country was poor, its infrastructures had been set back by about thirty years, and the level of consumption was very low. It was necessary, therefore, to invent something which would at the same time be suitable for the growth of the domestic market, the recovery of industrialisation, and the need felt by citizens for mobility. And just as Henry Ford had created mass individual transport with his Ford "T", so Enrico Piaggio devised its counterpart for underdeveloped Italy: the scooter. The relationship of imitation-diversification with the popular car (and even more so with the utility version) is a thoroughly conscious fact. For example, it says in the leading article of issue no. 18 (February-March 1952) of the magazine "Piaggio", which the company had started publishing in 1949: "However hard technicians and industrialists have tried to solve the problem of the utility car over the last ten years, this long-desired solution has always proved to be distant from the buying power of the majority of prospective customers, and even the most simple, modest, economical versions have been, and still are, inaccessible to the limited economy of most people. Nevertheless, the trend towards an integral motorisation has been increasingly emphasised among all civilised populations, drawing its strength from the increasingly pressing requirements of modern life. The need to master time and shorten distances has become a present categorical imperative, and the engine comes to man's aid to help him to overcome problems of time and distance in his daily toil".

The scooter already existed as a means of transport for airport personnel, and it had even been marketed commercially on a small scale in England and Germany. Piaggio decided to make it its basic item of production, and thus the **Vespa** was born. Its name was coined by the President himself: when he was shown the prototype designed by Corradino d'Ascanio, he commented: "Funny! It looks like a wasp!" And the Italian name of the wasp remained, and not "Paperino" ("Donald Duck"), as the designers had initially called it. The chief designer told the extraordinary story himself in 1949: the first article of the magazine "Piaggio" (*How the* **Vespa** *was born*) contains some interesting details about the passage from a wartime to a peacetime economy, the chronology of the development of the **Vespa** ("during the final period of German occupation, the technical offices of Pontedera, which had been transferred to Biella, had already examined the problem, studying the construc-

tions that then existed in the field of utility motor-cycles"), and its peculiar characteristics ("I took my inspiration for certain fundamental solutions of the **Vespa** from aeroneutical concepts, which were familiar to me, for example, the monotube support for the front wheel...")

The new vehicle was surrounded by an intense, effective barrage of communication. Initially, this was directed towards an adult public: workers, but above all young families, who felt the need to occupy their free time, just as had happened with the popular car in America, and even in the Fascist Italy of the "Topolino" (1936). Ford-ism *à l'italienne* had become a reality. The best designers, like the Frenchman Savignac, were summoned, in order to support the vehicle with mass advertising campaigns (which were not yet customary in Italy), and the product caught on at an extraordinary rate all over Europe. Highly effective advertising campaigns were invented, like the one based on the slogan "Vespizzatevi" ("**Vespa** yourselves!"). But the company also succeeded in creating a spontaneous customer organisation: **Vespa** Clubs, for example, with their own magazines and their own facilities. The family of products grew, on the basis of the idea of economy and freedom displayed by the leader vehicle: first the Ape, for the "workman's" transport of goods, as opposed to private transport, which was connoted as "wild", and subsequently the Moscone, or the sea-**Vespa**, with its buzz that is typical of motor-boats, but also with its strong appeal in summertime. Never has it been so true as in that period that *nomina fuerunt numina*: the names corresponded to mythographies, that is to say, "mythical compositions", dedicated to the creation of a coordinated image, full of contents, starting from the "family" names used for the objects.

The fact that the **Vespa** represented the redemption of Italian industry is clear from the pride with which the vehicle and its producer were presented abroad. For example, at the beginning of 1950, Renato Tassinari (the editor of the magazine "Piaggio") went so far as to say that the **Vespa** was one of the clearest expressions of the growth of our country, displaying in the process a certain attitude of *revanche*. "American, French and German newspaper reporters who had come to inspect the conditions of our country after the disaster of losing the war, have agreed that there are signs of a new vitality, and the impetus of a will to re-emerge is visible in many forms. One of these colleagues penned a title that is particularly significant for us: "A journey through the land of the **Vespa**". However, this patriotism on the company level was thoroughly justified: after five years of activity, the firm had already arrived at the goal of selling its one hundred thousandth **Vespa**.

The Vespa-rider: the last pioneer

The **Vespa** was already a great success ("More than forty thousand **Vespa** scooters are now circulating on the roads of Italy and several foreign countries", a company report of 1949 proudly announced), so much so that a "family of **Vespa**-riders" had been created. The sales network had also been developed: as a result, the decision was taken to try to "create a meeting-point between the producer of the **Vespa**, its agents who are following the development of the market, and the growing number of people who possess one". The magazine "Piaggio" thus took on a clear role of providing a link between constructors, sellers, and owners, in order to strengthen the bonds of this growing "family", thus offering consumers, too, the possibility of following "the development of production".

However, let us go back to the **Vespa**-riders themselves. In 1949, the birth of the Ita-

Following pages: Three pictures of a "masked" gathering of Vespa clubs in Madrid (1959)

lian Union of **Vespa**-riders was announced. About thirty **Vespa** Clubs which had sprung up spontaneously in various centres of the peninsula were linked up by means of a General Service Office, which took on the task of preparing the first Congress, at which representatives from all the **Vespa**-riders' Clubs were to decide on the nature and the organisational form of this new Association. Shortly afterwards, an analogous organisation was created for women. In issue no. 6 of 1949, the magazine instrumentally raised the difficult problem of the sex of vehicles. The author, Dino Falconi, asked, "Do vehicles have a sex?" In actual fact, the aim of this pleasantry was to introduce the news that the first all-female **Vespa** meeting had been held at Stresa on September 25, with more than 200 lady **Vespa**-riders taking part: during the course of the meeting, a certain Miss Graziella Bontempo, from Naples, had been elected Miss **Vespa**.

The **Vespa** had become a means of socialisation. As the meetings continued to take place, and the **Vespa** Clubs held their congresses, a photographic competition was also launched, and the best photos were awarded a prize and published. Insisting on this approach, another original campaign was organised. On Christmas Eve, **Vespa**-riders all over Italy took presents to the local police force in the big towns. The **Vespa** had thus been consecrated as a recognisable symbol of Italianness: joyful, popular, uninhibited, and substantially "full of kind feelings". As a part of this overall image, the **Vespa** even incentivated a return to popular forms of sport. (These included the gymkhana, for example: on April 4, 1951, the Genoa **Vespa** Club organised one which drew considerable attention).

The phenomenon of sociality, encouraged by the **Vespa** Clubs, was not only a means to find ways of exporting the product, but a strategy to plant the roots of the **Vespa** deep in the most varied forms of social and political reality. And the **Vespa** Clubs rapidly became an international organisation. The European **Vespa** Club was founded at Milan in 1953, and it included all the clubs in Italy, France, Germany, Switzerland, Holland and Belgium. Clubs sprang up like mushrooms, first all round Europe, and later all over the world: from Libya to South Africa, from Hong Kong to Thailand, from Peru to the United States. In 1953 there were more than 10.000 Piaggio service stations all round the world, and the **Vespa** Clubs had more than 50.000 members worldwide. At the beginning of the 60's, there were 220 **Vespa** Clubs in Italy, with 50.776 members. **Vespa**-riders travelled round the world, and their meetings became more and more frequent, with increasing attendances; "**Vespa** tours" began to be organised: the most important of these was the one known as the "Tour of the Three Seas", which covered a total of 2.000 kilometres. Exhibitions held at important tourist resorts, or in highly original places, were extended to include foreign countries, and the **Vespa** arrived wherever there was a collective public phenomenon : it even penetrated into the most tightly closed ritual world that can be imagined : "*en la plaza de toros*" (the bull-fighting arena).

Those, then, were the years of the greatest expansion abroad, and penetration into the international collective imagination. The **Vespa** was sold everywhere, from Brazil to India, from Australia to South Africa. And it could be seen everywhere: in songs (at least forty records contain a reference to the vehicle), in sport, in literature, and above all in films. This is the starting-point for another element of conversion into a myth, the "free" appearance (that is, not solicited, and without any immediate or evident aims of persuasion) of the **Vespa** in the common sense represented by works of imagination.

The collective imagination

It was through the company magazine that the first, fundamental element of the myth was created: the journey and the story of the adventure, which as we have seen, already existed in reality, as a result of mass tourism and **Vespa**-riders all over the world. For example, Orio Vergani, the journalist and writer, wrote a *Diary of the Vespa* made up of short stories, aphorisms and slogans. Here is one of them: "The **Vespa** stands to the big car as the wrist-watch stands to the old grandfather clock ticking heavily in the sitting-room". And again: "In order to abduct Europa, Zeus turned into a bull: nowadays he would turn into a **Vespa**"; "In two or three hundred years from now, when someone writes a melodrama based on our times and our customs, the perspicacious writer of the *libretto* will make the tenor go around on a **Vespa**. I can imagine a tenor of the year 2200 singing *Una furtiva lacrima* as he leans elegantly on his 1949 model **Vespa**, which he has wheeled on stage in front of the prompter's box". Several other journalists and writers subsequently devoted their energies to this new genre, which was built up around the **Vespa**, and scooters in general, as the main characters of the adventures: Corrado Govoni set his story in Rome (1951); Piero Balliano wrote a story set in Denmark (1953), while Jacques Provenza told a story of a trip to Cannes on a **Vespa** (1955). In the following years, we find Silvio Ducati's *Vespina and the witches*, and Aldo Manos' *Story of a giant Vespa and a Vespa that could be even bigger* (both published in 1958). At this point, the series of stories by Luigi Brioschi began, and went on for several issues: *The sun is there* (1958), *Schoolmistress on holiday* (1959), *Convalescence at the seaside* (1959).

Soon foreign writers also began to take an interest in the **Vespa**. In 1963, Maggie Vaughan, a young American writer, wrote a story for the Daily American Weekly, which was set on the island of Ischia, and described the use of the microtaxi (a cross between the **Vespa** and the Ape). Other works include *The Little Cabbages* by George Mikes (publ. Allan Wingate); *Vacances Romaines* by Odette Ferry (publ. Robert Laffont), based on the film, in which the **Vespa** plays the part of a go-between; *Ma Vespa Ma Femme et moi* by Daniel and Françoise Sauvage (publ. Gallimard), which tells the story of a 25,000-kilometre trip on a **Vespa** around the Mediterranean; *Rejse i Italien* by Tom Kristensen (publ. Carit Andersen Forlag), in which the Danish author speaks about his experiences travelling through Italy, and about the image of the **Vespa**, which is ridden by many men and women. The **Vespa** even ended up on the cover of a book by John Steinbeck, *The Short Reign of Pippin IV* (publ. Viking); the author had shown his appreciation for the **Vespa** in a conversation with an Italian journalist.

This, however, is the period of the beginning of an intense collaboration in particular with the Tenth Muse. It was no longer a question of actors and actresses as witnesses of the success of the **Vespa**, but of the **Vespa** itself that appeared as one of the main characters, or at least in a supporting role, in films. The first recorded case comes from abroad, with the musical *Professor Nachtfalter*, directed by Rolf Meyer, starring Johannes Heesters and Gisela Schmidting. The company magazine presented it as follows: "The Jung Film Union recently held a showing in Germany of the musical film... in which attempts at suicide, philosophy text-books and provocative dances in night clubs are set against a background of college girls chasing their young male teacher on their **Vespas**". At the first

Opposite:
The entrance
of a cinema
showing *Vacanze*
romane, **directed**
by William Wyler
(1952)

The sidecar
Vespa (1949)

showing of the film, which of course took place in Hamburg, the **Vespas** were proudly displayed. This relationship with the world of the cinema gradually became a constant in the promotional initiatives of the Piaggio company. *Vacanze Romane* ("A Holiday in Rome") was shot in 1952, with its famous sequences of Gregory Peck driving around Rome on a **Vespa**, and *Cani e Gatti* ("Dogs and Cats"), an Italian comedy starring a very young Antonella Lualdi and Titina de Filippo, was produced in the same year.

The relationship with the cinema developed all through the 50's and the 60's. Everybody took note of the **Vespa** as a typical element of Italian life when Federico Fellini included it in his film, *Il Bidone* ("The Swindle"). A magazine of the period wrote: "Everybody in Italy knows what swindling someone means. "Bidonisti" (swindlers) are a special kind of intelligent, amusing, and sometimes even charming con-men: they live off the honesty of others rather than their own ... The ones that Fellini has included in his forthcoming film, which is appropriately entitled *Il Bidone*, invent a treasure that doesn't exist. The chief of the swindlers is Broderick Crawford... and as soon as he arrived in Rome, he wanted to experience the intoxication of a motor scooter, the means that "bidonisti" prefer for their "activities" around the countryside, just like the characters in Fellini's film..."

Year after year, film after film, the **Vespa** carved out a role for itself, to the point where it has now put together an extremely important catalogue. Up to the beginning of 1962, it had already appeared in more than sixty films. In Italy, great film directors such as Fellini, Germi, Monicelli and Emmer have called on the **Vespa** to play roles which have sometimes been of prime importance, but there have also been many foreign directors that have used the Italian scooter for their scenes: from the already-mentioned *Vacanze Romane* to *Les tricheurs* by Marcel Carmé, from *No my darling daughter* to *Jessica* by Jean Negulesco, starring Angie Dickinson. At the beginning of 1963, the volume **Vespa** *in the Cinema* was published, in which there is a collection of illustrations of 43 of the approximately 80 films in which the **Vespa** had appeared. Some of these are extremely important: from *La Dolce Vita* to *Peccatori in Blue Jeans* ("Sinners in Blue Jeans"). And then, in the wake of *Europa di notte* ("Europe by night"), the film by Blasetti which aroused considerable discussion in orthodox circles, came *Questo mondo proibito* ("This world of prohibitions"), which used the same journalistic technique. In England, *Carry on Cabby* was directed by Gerald Thomas, and further titles include *Due volte bella* ("Twice beautiful") with Mia and Pia Gemberg, and *Gli amanti devono imparare* ("Lovers must learn") with Troy Donahue, Angie Dickinson and Suzanne Plishette. But the list is unending, and continues through to our days, with two masterpieces by Nanni Moretti, *Palombella Rossa* and *Caro Diario*.

Personalisation

We have spoken about the entry of the **Vespa** into the world of the common. We find confirmation of this in a reverse process of reasoning: the Italian scooter becomes so common that it begins to feel an increasing need to become unique and unrepeatable. The standard product becomes eccentric, anomalous and impertinent. Customers begin to change it in accordance with the criteria of a "mass aesthetics". The **Vespa** was immediately modified, amplified, and re-structured: the owners themselves added new elements, transforming it into another means of transport or a toy, or simply a means of personal aesthetic pleasure.

The first procedure of enrichment was implemented by the company itself, with the addition of a sidecar. Some customers had tried to make this daring experiment, and they submitted their project to Piaggio; on the grounds of the success of the project, the firm studied a model for the sidecar which would respond most effectively, in its attachment, its form, its weight, and its suspension, to the possibilities of its use together with the **Vespa**.

Originality is one of the virtues of **Vespa** owners, in their attempts to enrich it, transform it, and adapt it to their own needs and personality. The Countess Odetti of Marcorengo turned up at a **Vespa** rally, and was awarded a prize because her sidecar was particularly well-equipped: it "even had a radio".

The next thing was the **Vespa** for skiing. One snowy day in Milan, this sufficiently bizarre idea occurred to an office-worker who was forced to stay at home: the idea was immediately welcomed, and became a passing fashion. Small skis were attached to a normal **Vespa**, and it thus became possible to ski with a **Vespa**, and to use it to pull other skiers. (There are photos providing documentary evidence of this... sport).

**1956: The
Frenchman
Monneret
crossing
the Channel
on a self-adapted
Vespa.
Opposite:
The Vespa used
to break
the speed record
at Montlhert
(1950)**

It was not a big step from skis to shoes. A Danish shoe-seller built a **Vespa** with a sidecar shaped like a shoe, in order to publicise his little company. A photo of July 1952 shows him driving his son through the streets of Fredericia, inside the shoe.

The "seafaring **Vespa**" used by Georges Monneret to cross the Channel deserves special mention. This was the first time that the **Vespa** was practically transformed, at least partly, into another object.

A series of telefilms was shot in Nairobi in 1963 by the television company W.J.B.K. of Detroit. These were centred around the character of Bwana Don, played by the actor, Don Hunt. In order to be as far as possible in keeping with the character and the setting, the actor painted black and white stripes on his **Vespa**, transforming it into a zebra-**Vespa**.

Tommaso Fanfani recalls, in his book about the history of Piaggio, that in 1963, the Italian Army asked the company for a parachutable scooter, and that Lanzara replied that the version suitable for this kind of use might be the **Vespa** "90", with suitable modifications made to the back part of the body.

1967 was the year of the creation of the **Vespa** "Alpha", which was capable of travelling along roads, entering into water, and navigating. This **Vespa** was created by Piaggio together with Alpha-Wallis, for the secret agent, Dick Smart, the main character in a spy film.

The discovery of young people

At the beginning of the 60's, the Western world was shaken by a devastating revolution. The period of peace and expansion had created a climate of collective well-being, and consumption - as well as ideas - followed the same trend. Starting from the early 60's, young people became the protagonists of a world whose aim was social change.

Up to the beginning of the 60's, young people had only represented a small percentage of the Piaggio target. The message that was directed towards them was thus of a complementary nature. Interest in young people suddenly began to grow as their weight in overall social life and consumption increased, and also as a result of the introduction of a law which had a negative effect on **Vespa** sales. The use of a number-plate became compulsory in 1962 for all vehicles over 50 c.c. From this moment on, advertising had as its target the entire world of young people. Young factory workers and office staff, students, farmers, "all of them young working people who need a **Vespa** to move around"; young people who feel like enjoying themselves, "and nowadays the first condition for having a good time is owning a scooter". The **Vespa** responded perfectly to the needs of young people: easy to handle, safe, fast off the mark, and suitable for all kinds of roads, and of course, as everybody knows, "the ideal vehicle for courting couples".

Starting from this strategic basis, the advertising lines became even more clearly defined, developing a specific language for the different categories of young people. Mass schooling was spreading, and young students could represent an interesting segment of the market. Piaggio appealed to them by underlining their position of privilege from an anagraphic and social point of view. Students riding their **Vespas**, their eighteenth birthday, the girl-friend, the gift of a **Vespa**. Among the campaigns advertising this product, those conducted in young people's magazines and the sporting press were particularly important. All of them had in common the presence of a girl (a climate element) and a red

Following pages: During the 60's, new categories of customers and consumers burst on to the Vespa scene: young people and women

graphic frame uniting the images. There weren't any slogans, but there was a strongly explicit appeal to the fact that **Vespa** "50" could be driven by 14-year-olds and didn't need any number-plate or driving-licence.

The communication of those years closely followed the process of youth liberation, before, during and after the 1968 revolution. And in that period, one of the most extraordinary advertising campaigns ever devised came into being: "He who **Vespas** gets to eat the apple". This was an exemplary case of creative advertising: innovatory and bold in its language, in its image, and in its allusions to social customs. It included a bit of everything. Linguistically speaking, there was a trace of the *avant-garde* poetry of those years; from an artistic point of view, a trace of pop art, or American new Dada, could be seen; on the social plane, there was an allusion to sex and freedom. A new frontier had been created in mass customs and tastes.

The campaign was created by an art director, Gilberto Filippetti, who was then working at the Leader office in Florence. And the tendency to follow the world of young people's communication and figuration had already emerged. This found its expression, though, using the banal star system of those years (for example, the services of Gianni Morandi, the idol of screaming teenagers, were enlisted). What was needed, on the contrary, was a determined, breakaway campaign, more aggressive, or even transgressive. On that occasion (perhaps it was one of the first times that this had happened in Italy), it was decided not to make use of market research, and to plan the launch of the **Vespa** (in particular the **Vespa** "50") in a totally creative manner.

The basic idea was that of combining the concept of young people's freedom (the scooter had already been freed from the obligations of a number-plate and a driving-licence, and offered boys and girls a new, previously unknown independence) with the recent idea of sexual freedom. Nothing excessive, of course (the new **Vespa**-riders were aged from fourteen to twenty). And so, the new concept: eating the apple, overturning the sense of sin, to arrive at a joyful, happy transgression.

But the concept by itself was not enough. It was necessary to add a touch of linguistic and figurative anomaly to the ingredients. As for the language, it had become clear that young people spoke a separate language, full of slang, with a concise, innovatory syntax, which was influenced by their habit of listening to English in the songs by the Beatles and the Rolling Stones. And thus was born the fortunate asyntactic Italian expression "*Chi* **Vespa** *mangia le mele*" ("He who **Vespas** eats the apple"), with allusions to graffiti written on walls ("If you read this, you're dumb"), vaguely reminiscent of the behaviour of Giamburrasca. As for the images, pop art had recently burst into the visual universe of Italians, at least starting from the *Biennale* of 1963, dedicated to Rauschemberg and subsequently the one - even more pertinent to our case - dedicated to Lichtenstein. Apples were created with a bite taken out of one side, with their red colour and their clearly pop flat design, and subsequently they were varied in hundreds of other styles and colours, creating a multiplicity of variants which still today offers confirmation of the validity of the original idea. That campaign created a real upset in the world of culture and advertising. The left-wing culture, for example, which was emphasising its radically anti-capitalistic ideological stance, did not know what to think of the campaign. Advertising was an evil for the militant 1968 revolutionaries. But how could they help smiling at such an innovatory idea which went beyond all previous patterns? The discussions were unending. And they were also unending among the experts of the sector, most of whom were not used to the idea that campaigns could be devised without bearing in mind the indications of market research (it was only ten years later, with the Frenchman Seguéla, and the Italian Pirella, that this mechanism was given a theoretical basis). But from that moment on, the **Vespa** took its rightful place in the annals of advertising.

Women

Women, too were changing, even if at a slower rate. Firms began to realise this, and market research began to realise it, too, turning a fresh attention to this universe.In November 1968, for example, we find a significant move in this direction: a national conference was held on the subject of "The market and women", while almost at the same time, the CIRM Institute published its statistical findings on "Italian girls and the market".

Piaggio concentrated its own attention on these trends, knowing that in any case, women play a decisive role in the choice of the product. Recent advertising campaigns had paid particular attention to women, as subjects and as recipients of the message. Motorisation, especially the two-wheeled variety, was described and presented as a means of emancipation. And even consumerism itself was seen as a parameter in this race towards emancipation. Women and two-wheelers had already become a *leitmotiv* in the advertising of this period. Advertising had long since taken possession of women, and at the same time of two-wheelers, and in innumerable cases they were used as a support and a catalyst in the advertising of new products. The amalgam that was created transmitted an instinctive *joie de vivre*, inspiring psychological satisfaction. The best-known examples are those of the New York Stores, Peck and Peck, who presented their models sitting on a **Vespa**, Samsonite, who distributed red and blue suit-cases around a **Vespa**, and Algida, whose advertisements showed young women eating huge ice-creams as they raced along on their **Vespas**. And the same can be said for Coca Cola, Guerlin, and Pan Am, who made use of a pretty Polynesian girl speeding along on a *Ciao*. Enchanting sirens, tokens of happiness.

The discovery of a new world

As we have seen, the "communications workshop" of the **Vespa** has described a different world for at least two generations: the young, mature generation of the post-war reconstruction period, and the young, adolescent generation of the economic boom and consumerism. The world of the 40's was by definition a young world. It was just coming out of the war, with all its anxieties and hopes, and it dreamt of creating a modern well-organised country. It was conscious of its poverty, but during the conflict it had come into contact with the advanced Western cultures. And, as a result, it was looking for certainties. The **Vespa** was able to offer them: it provided a means of locomotion, and consequently private freedom for everybody; it demonstrated the existence of an "Italic" genius; it gave confirmation of the new status of working families with two fulcra. The Italy of the 60's, on the contrary, is the Italy of change, the one belonging to the children of the previous generation, who were free from the want of their fathers, and were instead chasing after the complete fulfilment of

pleasure, in a dream to be extended as long as possible in a sort of perennial Peter Pan complex. In this case, too, the **Vespa** offered the means to transform social imagination into reality: it was transformed into a toy with a real performance; it presented itself as an instrument for collective interaction; it expressed novelty, modernity, and anti-conformity.

We have seen, one after the other, the ingredients for the personification of these two worlds: the object itself, first of all. With its original, inimitable design, the **Vespa** was initially presented as solid (it is still made of metal, and this is not by chance), long-lasting, capable of courageous performances, and adventurous. In its second phase, it became light, colourful, joyful and easy to handle. Beside the object, the owners were correspondingly designed. Pioneers during the 40's and 50's: travellers, lovers of great exploits, chance tourists, tenacious and sympathetic. Innovators during the 60's: emancipated (girls, in particular), playful, metropolitan, gregarious, but with artistic tendencies. And there were consequent developments in the presentation of the product, that is to say, its communication, with a linguistic and figurative evolution that has seldom been rivalled in the history of a firm.

The present, the future

Twenty years have now passed since the end of the "young people's" universe, and we need to ask whether, and how, the **Vespa** can continue to be a myth for what should be a "third generation", the one that will be eighteen years old in the year 2000. Can this great little Italian scooter still catch on, among young people who no longer know what the 60's were, and for whom the 40's are just the last chapter in their history book?

Difficulties exist. They are clear, among other things, from the brusque drop in sales which took place in the 80's, in the face of a return of the favourite motor-bike of the Japanese, or the "sporting" character of cross-country motor-bikes. It is not by chance that Piaggio decided to substitute the **Vespa** at the end of the 80's with a similar scooter, not anchored to the past, the "Cosa". However, this operation was not successful, due to the lack of a mythical dimension of identification in the new project. The consumption of the **Vespa** over the last ten years has thus been a question of nostalgia. Again, not by chance, the old models - almost like modern antiques - are eagerly sought after. And in the world of creativeness, the **Vespa** is the object of the attention of authors, designers, and film directors, who are continually in search of that old feeling.

And yet the **Vespa** is returning today, trying to renovate its past glories. The ingredients exist. The tradition can continue, in its true spirit: which is not that of a nostalgia for the past, or the conservation of a fetish, or the memory of a past magnificence, but consists in being capable of maintaining its spirit intact, adapting it to change. Some lines of adaptation to the future can already clearly be seen: the theme of technological innovation, which makes the **Vespa** seem "revolutionary", as in other periods; its universal presence all over the world, like a kind of Esperanto among objects; its enormous environmental significance, in line with the common sentiment of modern generations. These are innovations that are at the same time tradition. Because they transfer the trends and the technical considerations that have always existed to the future. The new **Vespa** looks back to its past, but in a creative manner. It represents what may be called "the Utopia of the past".

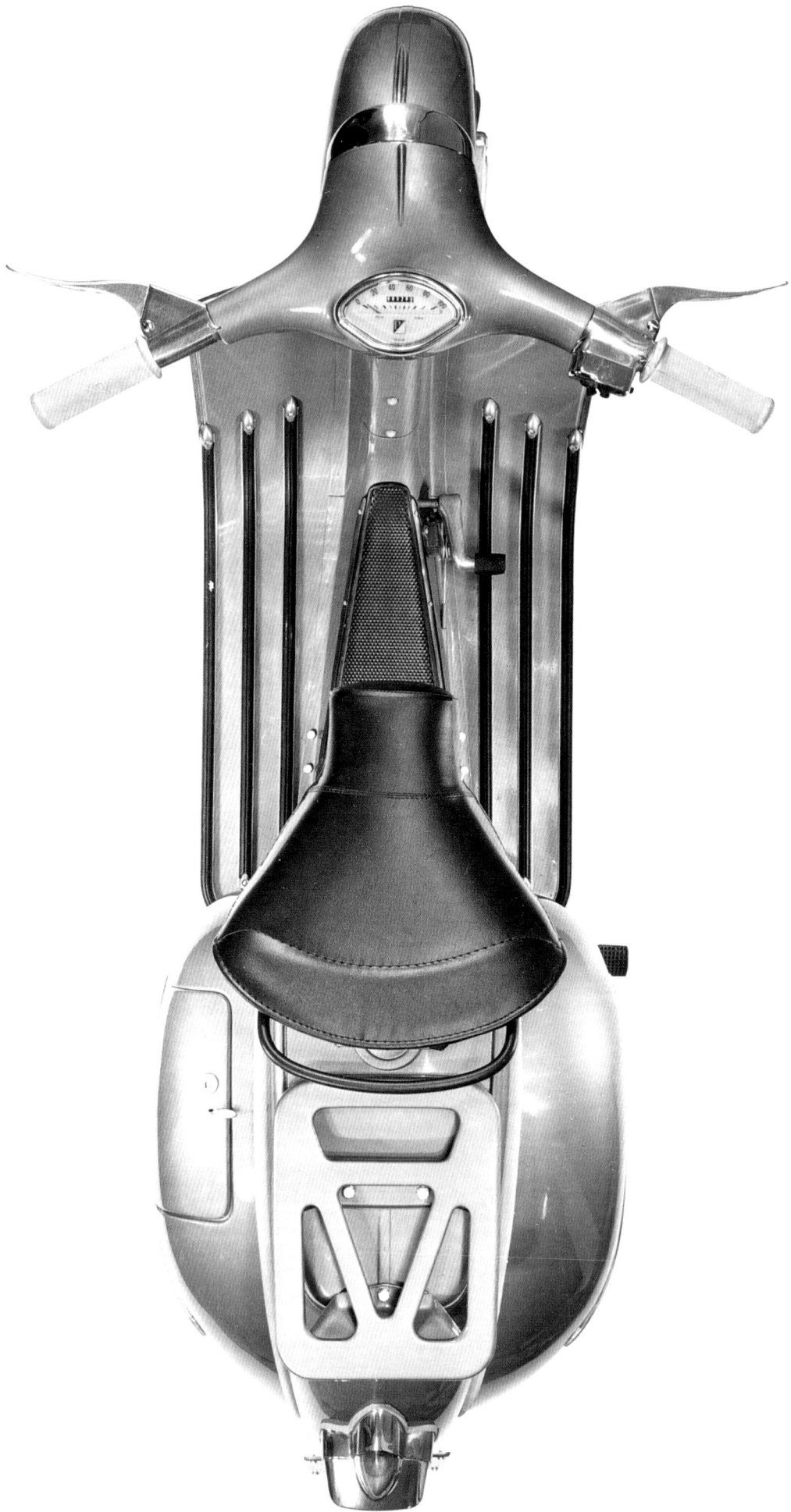

The "name" of the Vespa

Maurizio Bettini

What is the **Vespa**? A scooter or a symbol, a means of communication or an insect? ("vespa" means wasp in Italian). We know that semiologists and anthropologists possess the fine art of confusing us on the page in rendering complex that which appears simple - to our advantage, naturally. Otherwise, in this case as well, we would have continued to ride on our **Vespa** without suspecting that beyond our getting to where we're going, the sea, or work, we were above all winding our way through the plot of a very good novel (*see footnote 1*). If a real novel plot has curdled itself around the **Vespa**, let us treat it for what it is. We have decided to propose, in these brief lines, an imaginative anthropology of the **Vespa** myth. Stage by stage, from the birth of our heroine to the origin of her name. For in all respected myths, the heroine's name contains within it practically all her traits and all the adventures she is fated to face.

The birth of the heroine

Let us start from the beginning. We know that, in order to be a mythological character, you need to be born under extraordinary circumstances. The birth is, in fact, the moment in which the hero reveals himself to the world for what he is: if he or she came into this world in such an incredible way it means that he/she is definitely a hero. In the language of mythology the exceptional birth of the hero immediately signals the "fracture" created between first the brusque storm that separates everything that happened in the past era and next, that which the new era, signalled by the hero's coming into the world, now promises. Here we have children who have two fathers, or even three, others who miraculously escape from the evil charm which blocks their mother's belly; others still who, as soon as they are born, cross rivers and seas while locked in a chest, and still more who strangle enormous serpents without even moving from their cradles.

There are also characters who could be defined as specifically "motherless", those who come into the world as determinant apports of their only "father": like Athena, the goddess Zeus extracted from his own head; or Dionysus whom Zeus hurriedly sewed into his thigh after the child escaped from the pyre in which Semele and her house were destroyed. Here we are talking about heroines and child heroes, of pure paternal "bricolage". Being absent from a maternal figure capable of giving the child the substance necessary for the formation of its limbs, the fathers turn elsewhere for a surrogate for this terrible loss. And now here we come to the **Vespa**.

Which, in following the heroines of myths, also had a singular birth. And moreover her birth was all "paternal". There was no real "conception" of the new creature in the laboratory or showrooms; neither was there a "matrix" (thought of especially for her) from where the new creature could take the substances necessary for growth. Her limbs were very much surrogates, made of material which "the fathers" of this scooter found at hand, at times of necessity. Everyone knows, in fact, either by hearsay or historical testimony, that the **Vespa** was born from an assemblage of material originally destined to the aeronautics industry; the latter being readapted to their new functions by a touch of genius (*2*). But it is not only the materials that are important. In the new scooter, forms conjoin, which the motorcycle industry never suspected they could do, and which were subsequently altered by other engineering dominions: low wheels connected to a chassis which more or less was a

"... everyone knows, in fact, either by hearsay or historical testimony, that the Vespa was born from an assemblage of material originally destined to the aeronautics industry..."

landing undercarriage and came from the aeronautics industry; the main body, which covered the chassis and diminished dirt and noise, came from the automobile industry (3). The **Vespa**, post bellicose daughter of an unexpected "bricolage", had a miraculous birth on a par with all the heroines of myths. Chance and necessity, indigence and skill, united to find for her the "body", which the absence of a natural mother deprived her of. And this naturally signals her exceptionality, as much as the stormy 'fracture' was capable of signalling her coming into the mechanical world. All her success was probably already written there and then at her irregular birth: plus the profound transformations that this vehicle was fated to introduce, not only in the history of technology, but also in the history of customs and the daily life of our country.

A swarm of insects

The **Vespa**, our heroine, was the first born, naturally. But later she was not alone. Besides, heroes of mythical legends often share their adventures with personages belonging to their own families, stepbrothers, servants, squires. And so it was with 'Piaggio'. Almost contemporaneously with **Vespa** was born the Ape ("ape" means bee in Italian - *also see footnote 4*), the "work" version of the **Vespa**. Of this we shall speak of at length later on. Then there was the moped, the Grillo ("grillo" means cricket in Italian) which, it seems, did not have as much success as the **Vespa**: and the Moscone ("moscone" means bluebottle in Italian), a small engine destined to power small dinghies for recreation. To tell you the truth I had completely forgotten about the existence of the Grillo. On the other hand I do have vague memories of the marine Moscone, more of its name than anything else - a friend of my father's, for example, would call all the boats which had an outboard motor 'Mosconi' (moscone's plural - bluebottles). But maybe if I patiently rummage among the images and sounds of my childhood, I am able to hear the "buzz" of these Mosconi on the August sea. But even the Moscone had no enormous success. It was the **Vespa** and the Ape which lived on to populate our roads and, above all, our minds. Maybe this was to be expected. "Names are presages" said the Latins, "nomina sunt omina".

The "grillo" (cricket) is in fact a rather disagreeable insect, conceited too, as was the one in "Pinocchio". He makes us think of bespectacled, swotty classmates who would say things like: "If you play football in your new shoes your Mum will be angry." The same goes for the 'moscone' (bluebottle); for it does nothing more than buzz lazily away on some summer's afternoon and often creates only annoyance. It is a good proverb that says "moscone, novità o persone" (5), but frankly this is the only fragment of symbolic wisdom that one can associate with this insect. Too little to make a myth out of. Thus it was destiny (mythical destiny of "names") that made Grilli and Mosconi play only marginal character roles, squires and servants "a latere", in the mythical events of the **Vespa**. Wasps and bees are insects that have much more virtues, as we will see further on.

Here then are the **Vespa**'s companions: a bee, a cricket, a bluebottle. The conclusion we can deduce from this simple listing is already interesting. At Piaggio the engineers and creators (at the time called something else) or perhaps only a series of propitious chance impulses, weaved the thread thus plotting an extremely popular mythological novel about "insects". Why was it about insects as such? One is curious then to understand why this ty-

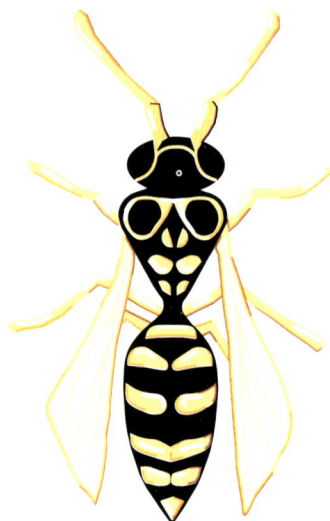

pe of symbol and metaphor was resorted to and not another. The first thing one thinks of, naturally, is the fact that those engines "buzzed", just as insects normally do. But this probably is not enough. When you are dealing with myths you must never content yourself with the first explanation which presents itself. Let us proceed with our investigation.

Above all we need to establish what image we have of insects in our minds and in our culture. The answer is pretty simple. They live in a society separated from animals or human beings, but with certain characteristics: it is a fast, small world which is made strong by their own weakness and, above all, by their speed. Insects go where humans and animals cannot, and often at such speeds that renders them unstoppable. For example, have you ever tried to catch a mosquito when it is not resting on the wall? Or a fly? Any human being or animal would need skill necessary to entrap one of these very banal flying beings - the problem is how. Flies and mosquitoes, or wasps and bees "scoot away" (this is the apt word) zig-zagging among every kind of obstacle without worrying about the hands stretched out to stop them. This linguistic image which has stuck in our minds of the insect that "scoots away" is extremely revealing. The word "scooter" is English and is used to indicate the type of vehicles that **Vespa** is. "Scoot", "make off", "slink away". The metaphorical ground completely emerges now; the vehicles produced by Piaggio are insects which, like good "scooters", "scoot away" - but where to? We have an idea about this and shall propose it, even if our reader has surely already thought of it him/herself.

The immediate reactions of our mind's eye see **Vespa** and her other Piaggio insects not only as "scooting away" along long country roads or suburban avenues (as did Nanni Moretti on his **Vespa** in the movie *Caro Diario*). Neither, and this regards the Moscone, are they balanced simply upon the lazy waves of an August sea - deserted, (we are in the fifties) - which unfortunately does not exist anymore. I do not know if they are conditioned by images of modern traffic congestion, but I can see these "insects" "scooting away" not so much "along" something, but rather "between" something: and this "something" turns out to be motorcars. Insects/scooters, this small independent society, elusive for its own fragility and lightness, weaves around cars like wasps or bees buzzing around big animals that try in vain to swat them with their tails. Scooters live, metaphorically, as if in the world of insects, for contextually they invite us to conceive cars as animals. Large beasts to fly around, zip in front of, lurch away from with a rapid beating of wings: a slightly ironic buzz it is, why not say it, like that of the wasp which flees from the movement of an impatient donkey. The epoch in which cows and horses, mules and donkeys roved our streets as means of transport is not so far away. Our Piaggio insects are a mythical metaphor built on that world, they get a kick out of reducing automobiles (this omnipotent presence in modern and post-modern times) to herds of heavy quadrupeds from which they can "scoot away" with a buzz. Oh, if only this buzz, so Italian, were a little sweeter! At least the **Vespa** has this merit, it is reasonably silent. But we cannot say the same for the myriad of "Moscerini" ("moscerini" means gnats in Italian) that populate narrow streets and roads of our beautiful country. If Piaggio were truly faithful to the original mythical metaphor, and would undertake to produce mopeds with an even more delicate and less penetrating buzz, they would be doing a favour to many people. At least people like me.

The name of the hero

But how did it come to be called: **Vespa**? In all respected myths the name of the hero or heroine is never secondary. It often is the case that the attribution of a certain name to the hero of a myth, and above all the manner in which this naming comes about, constitutes a fundamental moment for the career of the character. In studies by the Rees brothers, the celebrated scholars of Irish mythology who traced the ideal model of events necessary for a hero to be a hero, there exists a specific box heading: "the hero is given a name in peculiar circumstances" (6).

Regarding our Piaggio heroine we do know who gave her the name **Vespa**: and the circumstances were sufficiently singular. One is told, in fact, that the new vehicle was to be called "Paperino" (Donald Duck!). But Enrico Piaggio, climbing onto the neonatal scooter for the first time, exclaimed: "sembra una vespa!" ("It looks like a wasp!" - 7). A mere comment as it seemed at the time. But we know that, in myths, words fall much heavier than those in ordinary life. Hence the reason why it did not take long to discover that involuntary comment contained the true name of our heroine. So the scooter became **Vespa** and Enrico Piaggio's exclamation functioned as an omen in all its effects. What appeared to be a simple exclamation was in fact a phrase that had deep portentous significance.

Fate always has her reasons and very often these correspond to the logic of the culture. All "omens" have, in their nature, very deep motivations - Fate does not "speak" by chance. And so it was in the case of **Vespa**! This reflection brings us to consider an aspect of the "name" of the mythical hero which linguists and anthropologists have often given much emphasis to, that is its "signifying" character. The name of a mythical hero is hardly ever freely given or arbitrary. Oedipus, for example, had that name because he had "swollen feet" (or also because "he knew", depending on the variants); while of the beautiful Helen, who provoked the downfall of Greeks and Trojans, it is said that she carried that name because it contained the root of the word meaning "ruin". The fact is that, in myths, the hero's name is full of meaning, and this name maintains a deep tie with the specific characteristic of the person who carries it and with the adventures he/she is destined to face. It is not at all like this outside the world of myths. We cannot, of course, say that a man who is called "Arturo" or a woman who is called "Gabriella" immediately manifest certain characteristics: or that they "behave" like "Gabriella" or like "Arturo". "Gabriella" means simply "Gabriella", the identity of the woman who is called "Gabriella" is totally independent of the name she received. On the other hand an "Oedipus", or a "Helen" already carry in their name the sign of their own identity. What is the mythical meaning, then, of the **Vespa**? With this question let us draw near the topic (crucial enough as it is) of the "identity" of this vehicle.

Bees and wasps

The **Vespa** proliferated. As we all know she was followed by the Ape, a vehicle thought up for those new "insects" who not only wanted to move around but who wanted to work as well. It is, we believe, in these two names - **Vespa** and Ape - or rather in the fact that the **Vespa** was immediately followed by an Ape that an explanation of why Fate made Enrico Piaggio's mouth enunciate that particular portentous phrase "sembra una vespa", and not another. It is obvious that in order to face this question we must turn the clock back very far. Towards a symbolic logic of which the ancients were masters but which we moderns have almost all forgotten. Let us begin with "api" (bees) and so then arrive at "vespas" (wasps).

The ancients loved giving everything a motive. Thus they also had their reasons to explain how bees and wasps came into this world. According to them bees derived from a metamorphosis of oxen. Virgil recounts, in fact, that if one wants to create a swarm of bees, it is enough to kill an ox and wait for the flight of those enigmatic and divine insects to take flight from its carcass (8). This "ceremony" had a specific name, it was called "bugonia" or "nascita dal bue" (birth from oxen). Now we can begin to see clearer the reasons behind Fate's choice of names she wished to promote. Piaggio's Ape was in all effects a reincarnation of the ox living in our countryside. That tranquil, reliable, economical vehicle presenting itself as a peaceful transformation of the animal that had pulled the cart for centuries along long dusty roads and which now, in full post-bellicose technological mutation, continues its laborious journey with a push from a two-stroke engine. Maybe now our reader is already enquiring after the origin (according to the ancients) of the name **Vespa**.

According to the ancients this insect, which they held to be strongly related to the bee, had an origin similar to the latter: here again they told of the metamorphosis of a large animal, a quadruped. Not the ox, though, but the horse (9). When the body of a horse decomposes, they held, wasps take their flight from its carcass. The horse is certainly a much more noble and independent animal than the ox, it is the faithful companion of the knight who (after having bestrided it) roams through villages and countrysides. The horse is not shackled to the ground; is not a faithful servant who exhausts all its identity in its work. The horse is autonomous and realises itself in the freedom of its own movements and in those which its knight concedes it. The more one goes into this subject the more Fate, which speaks with the mouth of Enrico Piaggio, appears to be reasonable. For years, in fact, the **Vespa** took the form of a small, docile and bulky horse for millions of Italians. Just as the Ape was the reincarnation of the ox, the animal of work.

Festive oxen and wanton wasps

The ancients left us further information on bees/oxen and on wasps/horses, especially regarding their habits. Let's look at bees. Of them, it was said they were sober, chaste, faithful insects who hated strong smelling scents and the aroma of wine. Bees also detested those who had a penchant for the pleasures; so much so, that once upon a time they punished a beloved one who had been unfaithful to his fiancée. There is no doubt, bees are the true daughters of the farming ox, of the simple and slow animal who never betrays and who respects tradition. If we accept this logical symbology we must draw the conclusion that also the Piaggio Ape has been and still is a vehicle which represents simplicity and tradition, a motor which loves order and work. So much so that we are struck then by a phenomenon which would seem to clash in contrast with the above characteristic of the Ape. Ape: an extraordinary success in what seems to be Ape-Cross, a youth inspired transformation of the Ape of their grandfathers and fathers, the Sunday "amusement" version of the work vehicle of one time and today.

How on earth can we immagine an Ape - "il Lape", "la Lapa", "il Lapetto" or "Lapino"

Opposite:
"Donna in Vespa"
("A Woman on a
Vespa"), a design
by Leo Longanesi
(1955)

(these are all examples of Italians' pet names for the "Ape") of our countrysides - blasting out its stereo at full volume and hogging the highway from landrovers in an exultation of intermittent lights. But even in this case anthropological reflection gives us succour. The bee, as we have said, is the metamorphosis of an ox; but we know that there also existed the "festive" version of this animal. The ox covered with tassles and saddle cloths for Holy Saint's Day, the ox with its horns painted gold, while the band accompanies the slow march of the procession. This is true, there existed a working ox and a festive ox. And the Ape-Cross has shown itself to be the last flashing reincarnation of the festive ox.

Let us now move to the wasp. We have said that, for the ancients, this insect is the metamorphosis not of the ox but of the horse. Well, they also said that wasps, like horses, were bold and bellicose. We must therefore draw from this that also the millions of **Vespas** that have swarmed our roads have been courageous but open-minded too. A state of affairs which is probably true. The person who climbs onto a **Vespa** and not onto an Ape manifests at minimum his or her desire to be independent, bold, like the two wheels that take him "scooting away" between motorcars and lines of trees. But yet another characteristic of the wasp strikes us. Of her the ancients said that she was not only a courageous insect but wanton too, as much as the bee was, on the other hand, chaste and pure. This contraposition between our two vehicles - Ape and **Vespa** - is made even clearer. The Ape is a laborious vehicle/insect like the ox that reincarnated. Moreover, it is a household vehicle, docile and chaste. The **Vespa**, on the other hand, is an independent and courageous vehicle/insect which detaches itself willingly from the home and looks for adventure. And it may well be a vehicle no less inclined to wantonness. This last characteristic of the **Vespa**, true or presumed, as it is, is quite a surprising one.

If we wish to analyse this in detail our discussion should take, at this point, a further turn. We would need, in fact, to look at the quite unexpected topic concerning the eroticism of a scooter - if a scooter could be erotic, first of all, and how. But I think we have joked enough as it is. This "fantamythology" of the **Vespa** has already been pushed too far, and I am afraid that neither anthropologists not historians of custom would forgive us beyond our talking of a possible eroticism of the **Vespa**. Even if we would have our valid reasons for it.

How would anthropologists and historians of custom react, for example, if we appealed to the fact that the French name for **Vespa**, "guêpe", derives from "guepière"? A very strong coincidence; and even more undoubtedly exuding of eroticism. And then we would bring up the drawing by Leo Longanesi which portrays a **Vespa** with a lady upon it who has a slim waist just like a "vespa"(*10*): another metaphor fitting for our discourse. For, this lady has nicely shaped legs, and curves extremely similar, too similar, to those of the scooter she is straddling. This drawing by Longanesi could spark off further interest on the (as it appears) very feminine characteristics of this scooter; a **Vespa**/woman who could undoubtedly attract the attention of the public (mainly men) for which she was destined: but who, of course, today would merit a very different sociological reflection conducted by the lenses that the culture of feminism and "gender studies" have taught us to adopt when dealing with these subjects. Leave it be, our playful anthropology of the **Vespa** would either risk the paradox of being too jocund and too serious at the same time. Above all, though, as we continue riding along this road we will inevitably end up by asking ourselves: what did Enrico Piaggio *really* think when he exclaimed that ominous phrase "sembra una vespa"?

[1] This novel was written by Maurizio Boldrini and Omar Calabrese and is called *Il libro della Comunicazione*, produced by Piaggio Veicoli Europei S. p. A., Pontedera 1995
[2] Boldrini and Calabrese, op. cit., 21
[3] Boldrini and Calabrese, op. cit. 37
[4] This vehicle is a mini truck on three wheels. There is a single driver's seat and motorcycle handlebars for steering. Practically, it is a sort of Vespa attached to a truck's loading back.
[5] The buzzing of a bluebottle foretells the arrival of a person or news.
[6] A. Rees and B. Rees, *Celtic Heritage*, Thames and Hudson, London 1961, 224
[7] Boldrini and Calabrese, op. cit., 39
[8] Virgilio, *Georgiche*, 4, 281 sgg.
[9] Varrone, *Sull'agricoltura*, 3,6,4
[10] Boldrini and Calabrese, op. cit., 92

"... also
the millions
of **Vespe** that
have swarmed
our roads have
been courageous
but open-minded
too..."
Photo: Vespas
and Vespa-riders
on duty at the
Rome Olympic
Games (1960)

The History

Tommaso Fanfani

"If the Allies will not send us twenty million quintals (translator's note: measure of weight, 1 quintal = 220.46 lbs.) of grain we will risk dying of hunger!" With these words pronounced on 2 July 1945 during a radio speech the Italian Prime Minister, Ferruccio Parri, summed up the drama of the situation in Italy a few weeks before the end of the war. Most of the factories were unable to produce, the roads and railways were destroyed, the naval fleet had disappeared and piles of debris marked the spectral landscapes of the big cities. Vittorio De Sica and Luchino Visconti established stories of daily lives and with cinematographic make-believe documented the reality of a time signalled by unemployment, hunger and poverty.

Tuscany carried all the signs of the violence of war: the destruction of German divisions in retreat and the fury of the Allied bombardments had razed to the ground many industrial plants, among which, also the Piaggio factories at Pontedera.

Piaggio: men or products

Piaggio was set up at Sestri Ponente in Genoa in 1881 and had rapidly followed a long path of achievement and growth behind the push of Rinaldo Piaggio, son of Enrico the entrepreneur in the naval fittings sector, attentive to the introduction of technological innovations in productive processes. Rinaldo showed himself ready to expand his activity so as to be involved in all areas possible: from fittings for large steamships and warships he extended his involvement to railway constructions, first for the provision of sleepers, and then for the building of carriages, reaching such levels of elevated quality to win the race for the provision of the 'royal train'; a masterpiece in technology, builders' skill and cabinet-making. A participant of that generation of men who had "made" Italian economic history, like Alberto Pirelli, Ernesto Breda, Giovanni Agnelli, Attilo Odero, Luigi Orlando et al, Rinaldo entered the world of aeronautic construction while the great war was demonstrating the potentiality of this sector, then reached Pisa, where in 1917 he took over an aeronautics construction plant "boats with wings", i.e. hydroplanes. These were produced from plants in Finale Ligure and Pisa during the last years of the war and thus the level of the aeronautic construction plants ranked with Piaggio's achievement by now well established in naval fittings and railway construction. The history of this enterprise is the history of men capable of creating technologically advanced products: Giovani Pegna, Giovanni Castraghi, Corradino D'Ascanio were three aeronautic engineers who, from the twenties on, handed down an original project for the construction of aeroplanes, engines, propellers. Their work intertwined with the life of Rinaldo Piaggio and with those of the mythical pilots who tested out the products, who took challenges with adventure, who broke important records for the images of the company. The Second World War finds Rinaldo's two sons at the head of Piaggio, Armando and Enrico, who divided up their tasks: the eldest, Armando, had the control and management of the plants at Sestri and Finale; Enrico, the Tuscan plants of Pisa and Pontedera. The last war left the Finale Ligure plant and parts of the Sestri Genoa plant standing: the Tuscan factories were destroyed, in particular, the Germans mined almost all of the plant's pilons.

The "original" idea

Upon this scenario and with this history behind him, now with the fate of war appearing definitive and with bellicose operations still tragically being carried out, Enrico Piaggio decided to abandon the traditional productive activity in the aeronautics sector. And, in those years at Pontedera the four-part engine P108 was produced, one of the most prestigious if not "the" most prestigious great automobiles of Italian history; here patented propellers of varying flying speeds designed by Corradino D'Ascanio were produced; here radial engines were built, some of which in very few years broke twenty-one records universally recognised and appreciated for the company. The young Enrico had images of a destroyed country in his eyes, he understood the difficulties of competing with the powerful North American companies, he searched for a completely new idea to bring back the thousands of workers who, before the end of the war, were still producing; and to reconstruct the company for the market.

At his side were some very special men, like Corradino D'Ascanio, an engineer from Abruzzo and inventor of the helicopter; Francesco Lanzara, a Neapolitan engineer with an intuition regarding the company's organisation who Enrico met in Africa; Vittorio Casini, Renzo Spolti. These latter two, during the active months at Biella, where the plant at Pontedera had been transferred in anticipation of the Allied landing at Lampedusa, had designed and built a small means of transport, it was given the initials MP5 and baptized "Paperino" (Donald Duck) by the workers because of the strange shape it had. It was a scooter, a small motorcycle with low wheels, which recalled ventures carried out up until the beginning of the nineteenhundreds. In 1919 in Germany, Krupp had produced some models and had set up other companies in other countries like France and England, but no one had ever achieved success and the scooter in the United States was more or less assimilated as a toy rather than as a serious method of transport. Enrico Piaggio must have initially gazed with a mixture of great interest and surprise at that strange product during one of his frequent visits to Biella, given that it was from "Paperino" that the idea was born to build a small vehicle which was easily managable, low on consumption, and cost very little for motorising the country. The idea to work on the prototype was immediately taken, and Enrico, with the improvised determination and authority typical of his dry and solid style, sent a mandate to Corradino D'Ascanio to redesign the scooter. "I would like a vehicle which puts Italy on two wheels, but I don't want the same old motorcycle."

Intuition obeyed the prior productive request of re-establishing the plants, but it also put forward the target of social content: motorising a country full of debris, scarcity of fuel, without being able to utilize well-known schemes, but at the same time inventing something new, economic and easy to use.

It was the summer of 1915. D'Ascanio did not love the motorbike: he saw the limits of a vehicle with an inconvenient and at times dangerous transmission chain; he held the seating position of the motorcyclist to be impractical, he saw difficulties when punctures arose, in substituting the wheel; on the whole he found more defects than regards for the motorbike. In three months of frenetic work, D'Ascanio recounts, the new scooter, initialled MP6, very different from "Paperino", was designed and constructed; on 2 December 1915 the first prototype models seemed to be designed along a more or less definitive line, but

The prototype
of the Vespa 98 cc.
designed
by Corradino
D'Ascanio
in 1945

there were still many modifications and corrections to be made, especially regarding the engine. D'Ascanio had adopted certain "aeronautic" choices like the monotube support for the back wheel, but above all he gave priority to the elements of comfort and practicality: among these the construction of a vehicle that wouldn't create problems when one has a flat tyre (a spare tyre under the frame), the facility of riding it (wide handlebars with the controls at hand like a bicycle), a superb manoeuvrability in traffic, that is being able to ride it without ever taking one's hands off the handlebars; and finally care went into the protection of clothes from splashings from the road or from the engine by the creation of a shield and the positioning of the engine and gears directly onto the back wheel which was protected by the body-work. D'Ascanio united elements of practicality with those of easy means of use, along with solutions which he had found in his experience of aeronautic and automobile engineering, genial solutions for two wheels unthought of up until that time.

When Enrico Piaggio stood in front of the prototype MP6 and saw the very ample central seating part and the other parts thinner and when he heard the buzz of the engine he exclaimed "sembra una vespa" (it seems like a wasp) and the name **Vespa** remained.

On 23 April 1946 at 12 o'clock, in the central office of patents for inventions, models and makes of the Ministry of Industry and Commerce in Florence, Piaggio and Co. took out a patent for a "motorcycle of a rational complexity of organs and elements combined with a frame with mudguards and a casing covering the whole mechanical part"; this was the offical beginning of the adventure of the motorscooter **Vespa**.

The Beginning of The Great Adventure

The presentation abroad was immediately prestigious given that Enrico Piaggio, despite having pursued and embraced the linking of production for the popular diffusion of motorisation, decided to exhibit this "number one" in a refined, high society ambience: the "Golf Club di Roma" in the presence of the highest civil, military and religious authorities. General Stone, while curiously observing the flaming pastel green coloured vehicle posed in front of a **Vespa** for the American cinema magazine "Movietown", shook hands with Enrico Piaggio and congratulated D'Ascanio and his technicians. The journalists present also curiously stared at the **Vespa**, some couldn't hide their perplexity (and they wrote this down) as to its capacity of keeping to the road, dealing with hills, and accomplishing what the mandate declared by its maker said it could. Others were enthusiastic about the novelty of it and identified the **Vespa** as the first Italian post-bellicose product, almost the active testimony of the will for reconstruction transferred onto a national means of transport, as was - writes "Time" - "la biga romana" (Roman chariot): this analogy was prestigious given this recollection of such an element from a dominant civilisation. Every technical perplexity rapidly disappeared thanks to tests carried out on the raods which the journalists themselves could take part in and so finally came the pleasant surprise of being able to ride a vehicle which despite its small dimensions, despite the apparent limitation of the small wheels and cylinder volume, could face upto and easily overcome engaging slopes; show itself agile, easy to ride for everybody, for immediate use, and present no problem for dress.

The success in Rome echoes its analogous results at the presentation of the **Vespa** at the Milan fair in 1916. The Archbishop Schaster blessed the vehicle and Piaggio's stand became mobbed by a large number of visitors curious about aerodynamic and technical characteristics and form of the scooter.

The first fifty scooters were already ready, now the right path was needed for commercialisation. Up until that time the Piaggio company had operated mainly on public goods (aeronautics, railways, shipping) and so not only was the absolute novelty of the product very far from the tradition of the image of the company, but it was necessary to invent as rapidly as possible the road for sales. The first idea was that of handing the distribution over to those who already were operating in the market of two wheels; which outstanding model of Guzzi would promote itself as a winner along side **Vespa**? But the house of Mandello Sul Lario didn't accept the offer and Enrico Piaggio found himself forced, together with his most intimate colleagues, to rapidly individualise an alternative solution for sales not only of the first fifty models built, but of the 2,500 pieces on the production line at Pontedera for the rest of the period of 1946. The orientation which brought them to the choice of the "Rome Golf Club" as a strategic philosophy of commercialisation for the presentation of the first prototype prevailed again: in fact, having given up the idea of Guzzi, Enrico turned to the car company Lancia; i.e. a company of great class and prestige in the world of motorisation. The immediate commercial strategy adopted foresaw the constitution of the Society of Representative Agencies of Industrial Products (SARPI) of Piaggio, a means invented for the diffusion of the **Vespa**. SARPI stipulated an accord with Lancia in which **Vespa** could be exhibited in Lancia showrooms, where retailers were obliged to sell a certain number of scooters along with "Ardea" and "Appia", i.e. the most prestigious Lancia models of the time.

Reaching the first objective of the diffusion of the product's image on a national scale and enjoying a certain tranquility by the evasion of a productive flood, the commercial team of Enrico Piaggio created a scheme of payment by higher purchase for the scooter. Such a kind of salesmanship was not then around in Italy, but Enrico Piaggio observed the Northern American market with great attention and frequently sent D'Ascanio or Lanzava to the United States to study the production organisation techniques and commercialisation. The bond with the Americans was close and Piaggio obtained internal help from ERP, a powerful company, capable of accelerating production and answering to the increasing demands of the market. In fact after the first fifty exemplars were quickly sold, the image of **Vespa** and its commercial structure began to "go around rapidly"; in 1946 2,181 exemplars were produced and sold; a year later 10,535; almost twenty thousand in 1948; and more than sixty thousand in 1950; all thanks to its beginning to utilize the press acquired with ERP's funds. In 1947 the birth of the new model 125 corresponded with this diffusion and also little touches and continual improvements coincided with this time, among which the most remembered was the elimination of the control "rods" in 1951 and their replacement with flexible cables. Other changes regarded important technical aspects together with aesthetic improvement of the saddle, rather than of the front or back light, the lengthening of the footboard in 1951 to make trips more comfortable for the passenger, the introduction of a silencer and so on, in the constant search for improvement and attention to the public demands: male or female. The possiblity of motorising women was one of the main objectives in the choice of the shield: now whoever wears long skirts or well ironed trousers can make a trip on a **Vespa** with ease. Its success overcame all optimistic forecasts: Enrico Piaggio lived by now permanently in Pontedera and after a little while moved in to the "Villa Varramista". Piaggio's economic results launched Pontedera's Piaggio away from financial precariousness and from the uncertainties of the post-war years; memories of those recent hard years rapidly faded away from when Enrico Piaggio had to dip his hand into his own personal funds to acquire the minimum essentials of prime materials for building the first two thousand five hundred exemplars of the scooter. The Piaggio workers at Pontedera faced the social difficulties of the moment: despite frequent tensions determined by general political conflict among various components of the trade unions and, above all, among the latter and company representatives, despite episodes of violent clashes, they participated in Piaggio and D'Ascanio's successful invention. Employment figures and profits were very high; in a series of a few years the company became the most important metal mechanic industry in Tuscany and in the southern central parts of Italy.

The affirmation of a myth

The **Vespa** phenomenon became popular around the whole country and this popularity reached internation levels, beginning with the founding of plants for scooter productions in Germany, England, France, Spain and India. Its success was derived from the quality of the product, its originality, its reaching those targets of light mobility accessible to all thus encompassing the philosophy of Enrico Piaggio. This success self-fueled a phenomenon of diffusion of **Vespas**' image in part spontaneous for it derived from intrinsic characteristics and objectives of the product, and in part by an attentive advertising strategy. Enrico Piaggio himself had a good image: serious entrepreneur, esteemed, far away from the noises of high society gossip, capable of choosing his friends the same way he selected and valued his genial collaborators.

The next step was the creation of a large and festive commercialisation machine. Around the scooter an intense atmosphere of interest at every level was created, provoked by gatherings, debates, congresses. Renato Tassinari, sports journalist, ended up by dedicating all his resources to the organisation and diffusion of **Vespas**' image, along side the men from Piaggio. I don't know in which of those men lay the "baggage" of natural sociological awareness or the market strategies for 'caressing' and soliciting the tastes of the consumers, I know though that they invented a series of posters and initiatives around the **Vespa**, to the point of making it become a social phenomenon of national and international dimensions. Tassinari was the first to organise a gathering of "Vespisti" (Vespaers) for the occasion of the Milan Fair in 1949; two thousand people, many of whom were women, arrived from all over Italy unprededentedly creating a festive and involved 'silver swarm'. From then on these **Vespa** gatherings occurred with increasing frequency, reliability trials, gymkhana, initiatives which exalted technical characteristics of the scooter, its usability for living in freedom, for enjoying one's free time, for conjoining work and play, business engagements and competition, and simply socialising. The advertising creators' adhesive forms initiated by Tassinari and Barnato converged into the setting up of various 'Vespisti Clubs'. A form of identity was created for any person anywhere, with a very precise common denominator, "fight" to obtain the supremacy of the **Vespa** over all other two wheeled vehicles, and above all begin the battle with that other national scooter which has

Opposite:
A gathering
of Vespa-riders
in France
during the 50's

just come out, the Lambretta produced by Innocenti. These hostile episodes of competition between supporters of one or another scooter were very frequent in small towns and country villages just as much as in cities, the clash was about the supremacy amongst the two products of the time, protagonists of human and social events, of which only one knew how to defeat them and stay on to reach its fiftieth anniversary.

Many of the most important Italian cities were invaded every year by a pacifistic army of Vespisti, a coloured swarm which became the ambassador of important social values in a country, with outstretched arms for reconstruction, still covered with rubble. In 1951 around 20.000 Vespisti took part in "Vespa Day"; the "Giro dei Ttre Mari" (trip of three seas) - a run of 2.000 kilometres - was organised, " L'Audax femminile", the 1.000k race emulating the Thousand Mile Car Race. The **Vespa** thus became a national and supernational phenomena which, especially for Italy, characterised an epoch, a sign for more than a generation and found testimony in the cinema, in literature, in images and exaltations of those values which it solicited.

Along side the **Vespa** Clubs, which in 1953 had more than fifty-three thousand adherents, along side the gatherings, the company at Pontedera continued its competetive strategic actions branching out and rapidly consolidating its own commerical diffusion in its territory. In 1953 the number of Piaggio branches in the world exceeded 10.000; in the same year the **Vespa** was presented to Pope Pius XII; on the occasion, Enrico Piaggio gave the Pontefice a gift in the form of an exemplar of the **Vespa** "125" and the Pope entrusted it immediately to a missionary leaving for the Far East: The **Vespa** - it was written - becomes the instrument of evangelisation, but surely it will become the messenger of national creativity in far away countries.

In 1948 the production of the Ape began, the other product which immediately found its usual employments next to more extravagent ones, like the Ape Richshaw, the Ape taxi, like the postal truck and so on. The Ape contributed to increasing awareness and interest around the company Piaggio and above all around the **Vespa**.

Piaggio never sat back to watch and continuously challenged the world's laws regarding two wheels. In 1951 a prototype of the **Vespa** "125" was built to beat the 1kilometre world speed record: it reached a velocity of 171 km\h! The vast numbers of "Vespisti" applied their own hypothetical uses for the scooter: in 1952 George Monneret built an amphibious **Vespa** for the London-Paris rally including the crossing of the English Channel. A university sturdent Giancarlo Tironi surpassed the Polar Arctic Circle; the Argentine Carlo Velez crossed "La Cordigliera" of the Andes from Buenos Aires to Santiago in Chile; Giuseppe Morandi crossed the desert. Its challenges were innumerable and it is impossible to remember them all fully. Today Giorgio Bettinelli lives his life wandering around the whole world on board his **Vespa** "PX 150", symbol of the members of "Vespisti" who challenged any law of the time and who demonstrated the up-to-dateness Pontedera's interest had for its scooter.

The collective image has no limits for applications and constructions of the most singular prototypes, important directors used the **Vespa** for actions and scenes in films famous in the history of cinema, beginning with "Vacanze Romane" where Gregory Peck and Audrey Hepburn used the Piaggio scooter as a symbolic representation of Italy and initiated a long tradition which has reached us today, in particular - for example - the recent "Caro

**Opposite:
Two figures
dressed up
during Carnival in
a comic parody
of *Vacanze
romane*
(Valencia 1954)**

Diario" by Nanni Moretti. Cinema is certainly, today as it was then, a powerful publicity ve-
chicle, even more so if conjugated with an approachable and loveable story, and if upon
the **Vespa** highly professional famous actors and actresses are riding.

A series of factors and initiatives contributed to its rapid penetration into the market;
facts of individual inventions, unique applications and transformations, but above all, through immediacy and rapidity whereby the company managed to build an ample interest
around the scooter, an interest of a thousand aspects, exalted and produced by a masterly
advertising strategy. "Vespizzatevi" (Vespa-rise yourselves!) appeared in 1956, it was a categorical imperative and a genial find for inciting buyers to take part in a phenomenon, which had consolidated its social dimensions. The work on this publicity message capable of
soliciting **Vespas**' basic characteristics represents an element of continuity in Piaggio's
strategy, like the work on the creation of the calendar, often entrusted to important artists
capable of adding to the drawing or text values of freedom, socialisation, enjoyment, contact with nature, all contained within **Vespas**' basic philosophy and in its ample commercialisation.

The attempt of the **Vespa** on four wheels, however, failed: the **Vespa** "400", produced in 1956 at the Piaggio plants in France, was designed by Corradino D'Ascanio, but the
market wasn't willing to widen the success of the scooter to the car. On the contrary, the
tendency to widen the range of **Vespa** models until they arrived at "cinquantino" - **Vespa** "50" - (for the very young who weren't old enough to have a driving license) rewar-
ded their commercial strategy and, despite the cyclic set backs in economic history that
every company and every sector must periodically face, **Vespa** remained the satisfied
object of desire for men, women, and young people from all parts of the world. Only the
recent introduction of electronic scooters with furture designs and styles have modified
Vespas' position on the market.

The episodes that Piaggio's historical archives recount regarding the birth of the **Vespa** and its achievement are infinite; even more so are its images, its thousands of photos
or cinematographic testimonies of publicity campaings or of daily life, consenting us to follow the **Vespa** phenomenon step by step, its growth and its achievement among people
from all the social scales of culture, race and extraction. What counted was that in 1965, the
year Enrico Piaggio died, 3.500.000 **Vespa** exemplars in various models originating from
the initial 98cc were produced and sold. Today production figures have exceeded fifteen
million. With the **Vespa** Piaggio has been able to construct the wealth of he who designed and wanted it, along side the well-being of thousands of families who, in fifty years,
have lived through the **Vespa** phenomenon.

Towards the future

Today Piaggio is very different from the Piaggio of 1946, it is so because of the changes
within the working environment, for the realisation of the "integrated factory", the automa-
tion of the production lines, the substitution of a large part of human work by robots, the
construction of streamlined and aerodynamic vehicles and technical and mechanical characteristics far different from those of the first **Vespa**; but this is due also because "social"
rapports have changed: today the sourness of the post-bellicose years' clashes, the compli-

Here and in the following pages: "Vespizzatevi!" ("Vespa yourselves!") a slogan valid for life in the mountains, at the seaside and in town, in three postcards from the mid-50's

cations of general political scenarios, the implications of a cold war regarding companies' internal conflicts has disappeared or has at least been attenuated. The Berlin wall has come down, industrial relationships are more moderate. What remains is the dialectic among parts, a dialectic of which everyone is aware; but the pursuit of analagous objectives to those fifty years are retraceable in the genesis of the **Vespa**. I refer to the spread of well-being which then was translated as the attempt to motorise the country through a vehicle which was comfortable and fun, useful and capable of making the best use of time at work and at play. Also today basically the finalities of a "social" order remain along side those persistent "economic" orders, to the advantage of everyone: the search for a product which knows itself to be compatible with the enjoyment of the environment, which reduces pollution as much as possible, which consents the facilitation of light mobility in all its aspects, are, I believe, persistent elements which in this article at times I have called values.

It's true, we run the risk of hagiography, but basically we can ask: doesn't the following: the imitative processes where Pontedera's scooter has always been the subject in Italy and in many other countries of the world, the constant search by actors, directors, artists, writers of the **Vespa** as a testimonial of a particular phase of society or of a way of living in a society of yersterday or today, and the significant history and topical new of this motorscooter...amply legitimize a participatory reconstruction even emotively? Moreover, celebrating a fiftieth anniverary for a mechanical product, for a vehicle made up of different materials, is not at all usual and also the solicitation should not be usual: i.e. as the **Vespa** has been and is the precise reference to emancipation for both the past and the present, it still must be used for its intrinsic ends as a means of locomotion, but it can be an instrument of education for formation in work and in circulation for the young and for the lesser young, in one word it must be "charged" with that social function spontaneously conferred on this motorvechicle by the "Vespisti" and intelligently done so by its producers. The escape of Renato Guttoso's lovers is not a stereo type of a past time, but it is the happy image which knows not the passing of time.

The form of the Vespa

François Burkhardt
Francesca Picchi

The **Vespa** is on the whole a social phenomenon, a fact of custom, a symbol of our first economic boom, a portrait of the industrial history of our country, an industrial product having the character of collective enterprise of which skilled workers, technicians, administrators gave their own contribution based on a "cultura del fare" (a culture of making) acquired through factory work experience. The **Vespa** has introduced new and astute communication and commercialisation strategies, from higher purchase sales to geographical extensions of its dealers; it has experimented with new propaganda methods along the lines of American systems, from the initiatives of the **Vespa** Club which flooded the cities with a new generation; "Vespisti" (Vespaers), who belong to the nascent model of young people, to the more direct promotion initiatives of dealers dotted around the country (like the one called - "imparate a disegnare la firma!" - learn to draw the sign[1]) which encouraged farmers, who could hardly read, to confront the modern world by using a motorised vehicle. But the **Vespa** is above all an industrial product, born thanks to the obstinate intuition of an entrepreneur who knew how to prefigure the scenario for the light motorisation industry, and the inventive rationale of a mechanical engineer of great talent; both brought to fruition the qualities of a company with a long mechanical history, first beginning with naval construction, then railways, and finally aeronautics. At a distance of fifty years we can see a sufficiently detatched prospect ahead, the background of the war, devestation of cities, uncertainty of reconstruction, the conviction that the future must be rendered better (from the world's point of view of the project and the awareness of its own task, it is enough to remember the appeal to industry that Gio Ponte launched in 1944 in the pages of the magazine "Stile", in the light of the "cifre parlanti" (speaking figures) from which emerged the eloquent datum of 20 million spaces to be built: "a situation like this presented itself to an Italy that had no precedent in its work history: a colossal internal need, a technical, industrial and civil necessity to quickly and efficiently adopt without waste the vital parameters, unifications, normalisations, perfect production series, ….").

The arrival of **Vespa** "98" on the market in those years had a liberating effect also because it raised the expectations of a reassuring reality on which these instances of renewal could be projected. The **Vespa** was in fact welcomed as an object of "Rebirth", as a slow and serene sign of a way of building-a-new, which intuited the generous possibilities of history. As it has been observed[2] the impact that **Vespa** had on a psychological plane should not be underestimated when one is informed "for the first time in our country (of) the sensation of the reality of mass production". And in fact "the form of the **Vespa** was new and uniquely dictated by industrial demands (function, cost) and, as such, knew to impose "a design free from precedent".

In 1913, during the alternating events of the war, a Piaggio technical group was transferred to Biella together with some of the machinery transported (by rail) from the company's head quarters at Pontedera. The task Enrico Piaggio assigned them was to investigate new possible productive roads for an aeronautic industry which, with its difficult conjuncture, survived by producing aluminum pots while adopting a totally inadequate technology and a workforce lacking in technical experience. Among the products under research were a motorised shovel, a washing machine, both acquired in Switzerland, and a small scooter which Count Trossi di Biella, a passionate racing car driver, said he had collected from among the aids and supplies the Allies had parachuted down to the partisans.

Some of the historic models of the 40's and 50's confirm the extraordinary continuity of design of the Vespa. In particular, the back part of the body, with its wide curves and its sudden narrowing at the level of the seat, is clearly reminiscent of a "wasp-like waistline".
Photo: the Vespa 40 cc. (1946)

The "scooter-parà", probably the "Velte" Vittorio Belmondo, was the starting point of the formation of the MP5, a scooter nicknamed "Paperino" (Donald Duck), the direct ancestor of the **Vespa**, by the Piaggio group of engineers relocated in Biella. Unconvinced by the result, Enrico Piaggio wanted to involve the engineer Corradino D'Ascanio in the project, the designer of the first helicopter capable of flying which, at Ciampino on 13 October 1930, broke a record for height, length of time, and distance unbeaten until 1938. D'Ascanio refused categorically to be involved in a project not his own and wanted to start from scratch.

This confrontation with "Paperino" shows the substantial discard which existed in the resolved project of the **Vespa**, it serves to help us understand the value of an archetype when faced with some formal analogy. Corradino D'Ascanio posed the problem in absolute global terms, attempting to investigate how it would be possible to realise a new conception of a means of transport, and at the same time asking himself with extreme patience to detail what would be the expectations, the needs, not expressed by hypothetical means, to be translated into reality; all this with the subtle capacity of prefiguring things based on a problematic approach which, starting from the analysis of what had been done, rejected it, overcame it with a willingness to bring the existing product to perfection.

D'Ascanio's words are enlightening if we are to follow the line of reasoning which takes into consideration all the problem data, where every logical supposition is conducted to the consequence of its form.

"Not being a slave to motorcycle traditions, I thought that the 'car' should serve those who, like myself, had never been on a motorbike and who hated how difficult they were to ride. I began rummaging around a little and one Sunday a basic idea came to me, the most important question was to climb onto the vehicle comfortably, something that had already been resolved for the lady's bicycle. I considered much more comfortable and rational the seated postion over the straddled one, then one needed to deal with facilitating the handling control to its maximum. One needed to take note of the vehicle's use for the citizen, that one must be able to ride it without taking one's hands off the handlebars, I placed the gear-changes on the handlebars. One other thing: one mustn't dirty one's hands and trousers, one of the most common inconveniences of the motorcycle. So, my little motorbike had to have the engine covered, isolated from its rider, a unique complex with the back wheel. As a consequence of that I created the transmission without chains, with link-change included within the wheel-engine group. Another solution dictated by my experience in aeronautics: the monotube as a support for the front wheel instead of the forked one originally for ordinary cycles. And, prime novelty, I introduced a body-work which eliminated a system of tubes. Another demand: the spare wheel. I remember that many times, while driving my car, I saw motorcyclists at the side of the road at work with the inner-tube punctured and the wheel dismounted from its rim; I decided that, basically, a puncture for a motorcyclist shouldn't be on a par with a problem for a mechanic. I wanted my motorcyclist to have something in common with the car driver. And so I tried to create the simplest 'car' possible."[3]

This effort of simplification which D'Ascanio undertook in prefiguing a new means of individual transport expresses itself clearly, and the reason for its "messa in scena" (placement 'on the scene') is shown in the ergonomics of riding it. The gear-change/engine/wheel

group, a unique whole which had found the necessary contructs from among the scarce availability of materials, which guarantees total faith in transmission, in reality hides the precise intention of freeing that space (disposition of mechanical organs), which in the motorbike is occupied by the tank/engine group. This recuperated space, which above all offered full visibility for long distance riding thanks to the erect posture of the neck compared to the elongated position typical of the rider on his motorcycle (due to the fact that his weight was discharged, in part, onto the handlebars).

The **Vespa** was born from an essentially aeronautic conception, its designer was a pioneer in vertical flying and a refined designer in the field of mechanical aeronautics. The invention of a new vehicle for light transport appeared in a way conceptually diverse from the motorbike and not only for its frame which counter distinguishes it when compared to that trellis of tubes of its antagonist scooter: the "Lambretta". The motorbike was born typologically from the application of an engine to a bicycle which provided it with a central symmetric structure; it is from this hybrid matrix that the evolutionary process of the motorcycle took off, which with time has produced a stable and defined form of value. The motorbike, up until the birth of the scooter, was a vehicle for leisure or sport, it wasn't shaped as a real means of locomotion, it demanded a certain riding skill and a notable mechanical knowledge. The **Vespa** expresses a totally autonomous constructive conception which is understood considering its aeronautic origins, not only by its designer but also by the company which conceived it. The **Vespa** is in fact the product of a crippling aeronautics industry which up until a few months previously boasted productive rhythms of a certain grandeur (on average in a month Piaggio was capable of producing five four-engine aircrafts as well as propellers and radial engines). All this means being possessed with sophisticated technology and a workforce not only highly specialised, but also passionate and attentive, which expressed an attitude of reasoning in terms of reliability and safety; and in terms of a rigid and light body-work which produced maximum efficiency of air penetration. In fact the skilled workforce contributed to a project which absorbed them completely, so much so that in less than four months (D'Ascanio was called to Biella in the summer of 1945 and already by September the first **Vespas** had been tried out) it was possible to get ready a productive system which, given its inadequacy for a concept of such grandeur, allowed Piaggio to be present at the "Salone dell'auto" in Turin[1], already by the end of '45 to demonstrate the new vehicle in the presence of the Allied military government in Rome, and to file its patent on 23 April 1916 (in March the go ahead was already given to produce 2.000 vehicles). The words of the patent underlined some key points about this "special form motorbike" conceived in a way "in which all its mechanical organs are covered and protected and whose driving mechanisms are practical and comfortable for its rider". The object of the patent was said to be "carried" by a form which is structured in three main parts: the so-called front cover, a sort of protective shield against "mud and dust", the central part consisting of an ample, and therefore comfortable, footboard constituting an "organ of resistance and connection"; and finally the bonnet which from the footboard it "divides, curving upwards" and which "contains the engine, ventilator, wheel, fuel tank, etc...".

The lateral "fairings" function on the one hand as a ventilator cover and on the other as a "container for tools and luggage rack". Their "round bellied" and slightly streamlined forms, in truth, hide intrinsic aerodynamic planning regarding orientation of airflow destined to cool the engine down by being obliged to "circulate along a curve directed against the engine".

That poetic aerodynamic form, that the **Vespa** expresses more than an alignment of a certain rhetoric of speed in which scientific presumption raises it to the first construction of "tunnels of wind", was born from the attitude of thinking in terms of surfaces well joined together, of forms that defeat attrition and which demonstrate maximum air penetration, a mental habitus of a strictly aeronautic formation.

An interesting aspect of the **Vespa** phenomenon is the strong bond which ties the quality of the essentially artisan work of the matrix to the prospect of production on a grand scale. When Enrico Piaggio gave the go-ahead for the production of the **Vespa**, the company found itself in the position of recuperating capital to support the reorganisation of the plant which had suffered very serious damages, at the hands of both the Germans and the Allies, and that only in 1913 employed more than 14,000 people. With the capital it drew from the "Villaggio Piaggio mortgage" it could support the costs of the project and of the first series, in which the artisan component was still very high. In the first models the plate of the body frame was worked on "by hand" by sheet metal workers of great artisan wisdom, and it was soldered by systems which could be speeded up only with the introduction of "pin solderers" during the post-war years (still in the 1900's a **Vespa** needed around 90 hours of work). Following this, and while managing to exploit the finances of the plans for reconstruction, the plant was slowly reorganised and was able to produce a large series, while the coherent **Vespa** project remained unvaried. It needs to be underlined how much the project of this genial means of locomotion was not intellectually separated, in a material sense, from the part connected to the execution. The **Vespa** has imposed a brand new design which followed the laws of an autonomous development, resolved in the conception of a project which did not demand a slow process of sedimentation thanks to the extraordinary equilibrium it knew how to reach between technical facts (a two-part engine of simple and robust conception, "a game for young people", for those who were used to constructing radial engines of 8 or 16 cylinders), functionality of use and rationality of design.

[1] Thanks to a conversation with Francesco Bardicchia (one of the first Italian **Vespa** dealers) held in July 1996, we now know that the promotion campaign for Vespa, not yet well known at the time, was supported by most original actions, like the one of teaching the farmers how to sign documents by giving them a printed copy of their signature to be "copied" in case of need.
[2] Bruno Alficri, *1939-1959. Appunti per una storia del disegno industriale in Italia*, from "Stile Industria", n. 26-27, May 1995.
[3] Quoted in: Alberto Mondini, *Un'elica e due ruote: la libertà di muoversi. Vita di Corradino D'Ascanio*, Nistri-Lischi publ., Pisa 1995.
[4] From our conversation with Francesco Bardicchia we understand that, already in November 1945, the Vespa was present at the "Salone dell'Auto" of Turin in Lancia's stands.

The Vespa 125
(1948)

Once upon a time... the Vespa

Sebastiano Vassalli

Anyone who thinks of the **Vespa** today, thinks of young people or a youthful way of facing life; but it has not always been like this. During the bleak years after the Second World War, when the rubble from bombardments had still not been cleared away, the **Vespa** preceded and substituted the motor car as the vehicle of the economic recovery. The Italy that worked, therefore, got about by bicycle or, at the most, by **Vespa**. Among my memories of those years around 1950 are the exploits of one of our neighbours, the accountant "Signor Torquato" who had lost his job because of the war and made his living as a sales representative in the villages of the Appenines north of Genoa, between Liguria and Piemonte. Torquato sold products from dozens of small and very, very small businesses - jars of pickle, sodas, wedding confetti, candles and who knows what else - and every day he covered hundreds of kilometres on a vehicle which was new and extraordinary: his **Vespa**, of which he never got tired of singing praises, and which he treated like a human being. He talked to it, caressed it, took it apart from top to bottom when he heard it sneeze or cough (in that epoch the **Vespa** still sneezed, even though rarely, and coughed). Torquato's preparations for leaving, especially in winter, were much more complicated and laborious than those of a Tornado pilot or a Formula One driver, and they would take place sometimes at home and sometimes outside. What took place at home was the hero's "Ceremony of Vestments", with his newspaper - "Il Secolo XIX" - tucked between his shirt and pullover, a scarf under his raincoat to protect his bronchials and another scarf wrapped around his neck to protect his throat, a leather cap with earflaps tied to his chin, goggles, gloves... The starting of his engine was achieved, however, in the courtyard in the presence of a small crowd of relatives, young neighbours, the curious and dogs, until Torquato finally set off to face the world. And those of us who were there understood that he was off to fight against a mysterious and terrible enemy: "Signor Spada"! ("spada" means sword in Italian). At the time I was at middle school, and the struggle for survival between Signor Torquato and Signor Spada was as exciting and dramatic as the battle between Hector and Achilles in the "Iliad" or between Ulysses and Polyphemus in the "Odyssey". Signor Spada was a sales representative who sold more or less the same things as Signor Torquato and in the same mountain passes, and this fact was sufficient for me to see him in a sinister light: with all the space in the world - I asked myself - couldn't he have gone and sold his wares in some other place, where he wouldn't annoy anyone? Moreover, he was not even a local. He was from Rome, arrogant and overbearing like everyone from Rome (at least that's what our neighbour said) and he even had a motor car: a Fiat "Topolino" (Mickey Mouse!) which he showed off as if it were a Cadillac.

The "epic" of the two sales representatives, in the block of council-owned flats where we lived, came to be a "grown-up affair", in the sense that no-one spoke to us youngsters about it, and so in order to keep up with the development of the story we had to listen to the gossip of grown-ups. Signor Spada - said the wife and other relatives of Signor Torquato, when they met our parents on the steps - was a scoundrel, who would have done anything, even the most vile, to snatch a client or an order from the competition: but luckily, "Someone" up there was awake. God in person took the trouble to castigate this wicked creature who, with the involvement of the "Eternal Father" in this affair, (of this there seemed no doubt) had an almost uninterrupted series of damages to his car which caused him to waste precious time and lose money and which, at least at the time, had thrown

The Vespa 48 cc.
(1955)

to the winds his plans to ruin his rival, forcing him to change his job and home. For some months the "war bulletin" of the condominum recorded one victory after the other for our accountant and his **Vespa**. Spada - gossip said - had been seen up one of the most impervious passes of the Appenines trying to come to grips with a car that smoked like a steam train and refused to start. He had lost such and such a client in such and such a place because he did not arrive in time to take his orders; and so on. Later, though, the tables of fortune regarding this duel were turned around the other way. Torquato ran over a cat with his back wheel ("a black cat!") and had to stay with his leg up in traction for forty days, while his rival re-established his hitherto lost clients one by one and also picked up new ones. The struggle between the two sales reps was on again, without the exclusion of blows: until one day, up there in the mountains, something happened which would have even pleased the great Homer, if cars and **Vespas** had existed in his time, which repaid our champion of all the pains borne up until that moment. One December morning, because of the ice, Spada's "Topolino" skidded off the road: it overturned, its doors flung open and the driver ended up in compost heap, then a common sight, of cow dung. As fate would have it, the first passer-by to come to the scene of the accident was our accountant Torquato; who, seeing the overturned car and his enemy lying on the ground, stopped, put the **Vespa** on its stand, and went to the field to help him. He picked him up, while the other moaned and cursed against adverse fortune:

"I am delighted", he said, pointing at the dung in which his enemy was in up to his neck, "to see you finally in your natural element..."

This all happened in Italy at the beginning of the fifties, when motorcars were few and far between and the **Vespa**, to the eyes of the world, was the symbol of our industry and of our willingness to be reborn. Then came the "economic boom" and we became rich; but that is another matter and I will recount it another time with another story.

The consumer revolution

Francesco Alberoni

That which we call a myth is always the product of powerful political, economic, technological, cultural forces. It is the collective reply, choral and synthetic to an essential problem of that epoch. It is the form of a successful way of life, a desired way of being, of new potential. It provides a series of values, hopes, emotions. At times it manifests itself in the form of a person: a charismatic leader, a consacrated artist, a film star. But it could also be a monument, like the Eiffel Tower, the Statue of Liberty. Other times it incarnates in an object of common usage like the car, the phone, the cinema, the fridge, the television, the jeans, a scooter, a personal computer, a cellular phone.

The success of the **Vespa** and its myth can only be understood in the light of the great socio-cultural transformation in Italy during the post-war years; with its internal migrations, the bursting out of entrepreneurialism and the expolsion of consumer goods. In one decade, between 1945, the year of the end of the conflict, and 1955, the country did not only develop economically and limit itself to looking after the wounds of war. It underwent a metamorphosis. Its countryfolk, asleep for centuries, woke up. The individual, who had always been integrated into his community, family, church, guided by age old customs, shook himself out of it and searched for his own personal path.

Everything began with an unusual, and extraordinary political situation. Italy, in fact, had entered the war on the side of Germany and had fought against the Anglo-Americans. But, in its entirety, the Italian population had never wanted war and never loved being a part of the German alliance. At a certain point fascism was demolished and a separate peace was signed. The Germans reacted by freeing Mussolini and creating a fascist republic. But this did not get the support of the people. The enormous majority of Italians sided with the Allies and, when the latter finally arrived, they acclaimed them as liberators. The Italians did not feel defeated but victorious. The end of fascism and its myths coincided, as well, with a sort of visceral and definitive refusal of nationalism and bellicosity. This postwar cultural climate was very different from that of the First World War, made up of rancor, tensions and vindications. The country had turned over a new page, it did not wish to think about the past. It looked only towards the future. It was happy, full of life and hope.

What woke the country up to itself and to the rest of the world were not sociologists or economists. It was the cinema which, in its first phase, "neorealism", showed the hard face of war, oppression, poverty, backward times. But which, in such little time, mirrored the extraordinary will to live of Italians, their fresh optimism, their many hopes. It revealed a populus which was mild, kind, sentimental, which after the war regained faith in itself, in its creativity. Think of films like *Pane, amore e fantasia* (Bread, love and fantasy). *Poveri ma belli* (Poor but beautiful). Italians are mirrored in their actors and in their beautiful actresses whom they will love for a long time: De Sica, Loren, Lollobrigida, Gassman, Walter Chiari, Tognazzi, Mastroianni. Also the minor actors: Silvana Pampanini, Renato Salvatori, Marisa Allasio, Maurizio Arena. The American stars had always presented us with far away figures, inaccessible. Greta Garbo, Fred Astaire and Ginger Rogers, Humphrey Bogart and Rita Hayworth were not similar to us and did not give us any helpful hints for our lives. But Gina Lollobrigida, who played the "bersagliera", and Sophia Loren who played the pizzamaker, did. For this reason they immediatley became "objects" to identify with, models of behaviour.

When the Allied troops arrived, the Italians welcomed them with their arms open, with

Opposite:
Vittorio
Gassman

warmth and sympathy. It was the first sign of an opening up of the world, after the closed years of fascism. Italy, as well as having deep traditions and well-rooted values, was now open, hospitable, versatile, adaptable. In little time Rome became, for the Americans, what Paris had been after the First World War. A place where one lives well, where one can have a good time, where there is more freedom, permissiveness, whether one goes there for work or a holiday. The city became the second world cinema capital after Hollywood. Via Veneto, after a few years, became the recognised centre of what became known throughout the whole world as, "la Dolce Vita".

And we soon felt the demonstrative effects of the world of the American life, of the value of "benessere" (wellbeing), a cultural category that had never been that important in Italy before. It had not existed in the free world because it was reserved for the élite. And it had not existed during fascism, because the economy was geared towards the war and proposed a spartan lifestyle. To the question "do you want butter or cannons?", even against their will the Italians learnt to reply "cannons". But now, with fascism vanished, and Italy being an integral part of the great Western economic family, finally they could all begin to think again of butter, even if the two dominating ideologies at the time, catholic and communist, did not agree with one another.

The culture of wellbeing, the development of consumer goods in our country, were possible because they neutralized the above ideologies, thus setting politics apart. The public's behaviour regarding consumption of these products never followed the political differences of the two ideologies. The farmers who would vote for the Christian Democratic party, people form Biella, Venice, Trento, wanted a modern kitchen with a fridge, and a wax floor dining room with a television, just like the Emilian communists and the Neapolitans who voted for Lauro.

But Italy was still prevalently agricultural, with half of the population who could not read, with 45% of the above-said working in the fields. It still was not in possession of consumer goods industries, for its previous economic political program had never considered them important, and the political and economic élites of the time obstructed their arrival. They believed that economic development would have to follow the stages undergone in those countries with established industrialisation. First agriculture, then heavy industry and finally, only at the very end, the light industry of consumer goods. One wouldn't have thought that economic development began with the **Vespa** and "Lambretta", "Ignis" refrigerators, cinema and television. Even in 1963, Ugo La Malfa opposed the development of colour television because he was convinced it would have absorbed too many resources necessary for needier productive activities.

Italy succeeded in undergoing economic development because Italians did not follow the instructions of their leaders and intellectuals, but set out to produce consumer goods and buy them voraciously. And since no-one understood what was happening, when it was realised that the country was developing at an extremely elevated pace, they began to talk of the "boom". But, for the time being, the rapid diffusion of modern consumer goods like television, was not understood and provoked all sorts of criticism. By the end of the fifties this joke was still going around: "A woman in tatters walks along the road with two children crying. A gentleman goes up to her and asks her why they are crying. «Because they are hungry» replies the mother. «But, is your husband unemployed?» asks the man.

Following pages: Views of the inside and outside of the Piaggio factory at Pontedera during the 60's

The Vespa 50:
"a spiritual youth"

«No» - replies the woman, «he works, but we have to pay our television rental»". Obvious example of a rash attitude, an irresponsible dependence on the consumer society.

However, this joke communicated a profound truth. That people were more hungry for information, involvement, hope, than for food. They were ready to leave the old world, and emigrate. People bought televisions because they wanted to take part in a wider reality and leave the narrow world in which they felt prisoners. They wanted to see, evade, dream, desire. What, from an economic point of view, was a development of consumer goods, was from a sociological and cultural standpoint, a great collective procession, a generalized refusal of poverty, and of the old fashioned world of the agricultural farmer. Thousands and thousands of people moved from the South to the North, from the country to the city. Not in search of a fortune with which to later return to their adored little villages. No. But why didn't they want to have anything to do with them. Why did they prefer the cities. Women expressed it explicitly: we don't want to marry peasant farmers anymore. They wanted to go to the city, they wanted a husband with a secure job, they wanted to work in factories, they wanted a dignified house, with waxed floors and domestic appliances. They wanted a school for their own children. They wanted what was considered a basic right for everyone, which I have called "goods of citizenship".

Let us remember that Italy has always been highly urbanised. She is constellated by thousands and thousands of towns, which in the past, became flowering Greek, Etruscan and Phoenician city states, then Roman municipals, then Byzantine dominions, or important medieval fiefdoms, then free communities, capitals of lords, of emperors. And which, in the course of thousands of years and with occupation by foreign countries, became run down, impoverished, isolated from one to the other, ruralised. Then, with the people's reawakening, came the birth of the desire for an urban life. Everyone wanted to break from their isolation. Everyone wanted to return to being in contact with others, moving freely.

Studies on the diffusion of consumer goods inform us with extreme clarity what precisely the desires, the needs and projects of the time are. Consumer products are practical and symbolic solutions to problems. And in the fifties, people wanted a motorized form of transport. It was an implacable desire, a "good of citizenship".

But was this desire realised in a country with no asphalt roads, a country whose motor-car industry produced a few thousand exemplars a year, where the motorcar was still a luxury good, reserved for the élite? The car, in Europe, had always been and was still at the time, a luxury good. It was for those in possession of wealth and power. Cars would thunder past common people on bicycles or on foot, signalling the difference in status, power and race. Like self-propelled castles, protecting their occupants from the profane glances of sometimes hate, sometimes reverence. Not even the totalitarian fascist or communist regimes could come up with the production of a motorcar for the masses, for everybody, as Ford had done. For, deep down, they preferred public transport which was bureaucratic, regulated, and feared individual means of transport were too anarchistic, too independent. For with a private vehicle the owner can go wherever he wishes, according to his whim, and escape the control of the collective, of the state.

And so it was that Italians were able to accomplish something extraordinary, without precedent in other countries: they did not adopt the previous model of motorisation established for the car. They invented a completely original and new one.

Already by the end of the war, when the only mean of transport was the bicycle, they found a way of applying a small 50cc engine to it, thus creating the motorised bicycle: "il Cucciolo della Ducati" (Ducati's Puppy-dog). In a few years the entire country had accomplished motorisation in minature. The next stage of this alternative motorisation model was represented by the scooter: "Lambretta" and **Vespa**. Their success was explosive. All consumer goods which respond to a historical need are propagated in a very short time and win over the whole population.

The scooter, from the point of view of status, was opposite to the motorcar. It didn't differentiate, it didn't create hierarchies, it "equalled". Everybody could own and ride on it, males, females, young people, the old, the rich, the poor. The symbol it stood for in the motor industry was the same as the one jeans would one day stand for in the clothing industry. It symbolised equality for everybody, open possibilites for everybody. The swarms of **Vespas** on the roads told everyone, in the immediate language of material symbols, that they were free, equal and had all possibilities open in front of them. That they were a new populus, the young.

The scooter was not even a motorbike, it was not as uncomfortable, powerful or aggressive. It was a domestic object, manageable, handy, which could carry out many things. And among all scooters, the one most characteristic, most typical was the **Vespa**. Feminine, plump, but fast, dashing. The **Vespa**, even in its name ("vespa" means wasp in Italian), is a free insect, which does not have to produce honey like a bee, but flies where it wishes, on a whim and knows how to defend its freedom with a sting. The **Vespa** renders us freer from timetables and regulations. Riding festively along all the roads, overcoming all the cultural ideological barriers, renders you irrecoverable from all the secret policing of the family, the church, the state. With the **Vespa** you can do everything: work, play, travel, make love.

This freedom from status symbols, from wealth and power, social control, tradition, this spiritual youth, came to be seen also abroad thanks most of all to the cinema. Think of *Vacanze Romane* with Gregory Peck and Audrey Hepburn. But, since almost all the great stars of Hollywood came to Italy for tourism or for work, one way or the other they all ended up being drawn to the **Vespa** and had themselves photographed riding one. So it is that the **Vespa** ends up by symbolizing, for the whole world, a joyous life of freedom, not weighed down by status rivalry, money or power. The life of simple and happy people. And in that way it became a myth.

**Opposite:
William Holden
during the
shooting of the
film "The World
of Suzie Wong"**

83

Mars

Avril

D	L	M	M	J	V	S
				1	2	3
4	5	6	7	8	9	10
11	12	13	14	15	16	17
18	19	20	21	22	23	24
25	26	27	28	29	30	31

1951

D	L	M	M	J	V	S
1	2	3	4	5	6	7
8	9	10	11	12	13	14
15	16	17	18	19	20	21
22	23	24	25	26	27	28
29	30					

The passing of time

Over the years,
the Piaggio calendars
have reflected events
surrounding the history
of the Vespa. From
the early attempts
to break through on
an international scale,
drawn in the inimitable
style of Franco Mosca,
to the numerous
well-known faces (still
a "peaches and cream"
sensuality) who
accompanied
its development during
the 60's, and on to
the artistic photos
of Tam Fagiuoli
and Uwe Ommer, who
immortalised the arrival
of its maturity during
the 70's and 80's.
Pictures that have helped
to project the Vespa
forward towards
its future.

Drawings by
Franco Mosca

1951

novembre

D		4	11	18	25
L		5	12	19	26
M		6	13	20	27
M		7	14	21	28
G	1	8	15	22	29
V	2	9	16	23	30
S	3	10	17	24	

1956

luglio

D	1	8	15	22	29
L	2	9	16	23	30
M	3	10	17	24	31
M	4	11	18	25	
G	5	12	19	26	
V	6	13	20	27	
S	7	14	21	28	

settembre

D	L	M	M	G	V	S
	1	2	3	4	5	6
7	8	9	10	11	12	13
14	15	16	17	18	19	20
21	22	23	24	25	26	27
28	29	30				

1958

novembre

D	L	M	M	G	V	S
1	2	3	4	5	6	7
8	9	10	11	12	13	14
15	16	17	18	19	20	21
22	23	24	25	26	27	28
29	30					

dicembre

D	L	M	M	G	V	S
		1	2	3	4	5
6	7	8	9	10	11	12
13	14	15	16	17	18	19
20	21	22	23	24	25	26
27	28	29	30	31		

1959

92

FEBBRAIO

D	L	M	M	G	V	S
		1	2	3	4	5	6
7	8	9	10	11	12	13
14	15	16	17	18	19	20
21	22	23	24	25	26	27
28	29					

GIUGNO

D	L	M	M	G	V	S
			1	2	3	4
5	6	7	8	9	10	11
12	13	14	15	16	17	18
19	20	21	22	23	24	25
26	27	28	29	30		

1960

LUGLIO

D	L	M	M	G	V	S
						1
2	3	4	5	6	7	8
9	10	11	12	13	14	15
16	17	18	19	20	21	22
23 30	24 31	25	26	27	28	29

DICEMBRE

D	L	M	M	G	V	S
					1	2
3	4	5	6	7	8	9
10	11	12	13	14	15	16
17	18	19	20	21	22	23
24 31	25	26	27	28	29	30

Ornella Vanoni
Anna Maria
Ferrero

1962

Alu Ferrero

GIUGNO

D	L	M	M	G	V	S
		1	2	3	4	5	6
7	8	9	10	11	12	13
14	15	16	17	18	19	20
21	22	23	24	25	26	27
28	29	30				

LUGLIO

D	L	M	M	G	V	S
			1	2	3	4
5	6	7	8	9	10	11
12	13	14	15	16	17	18
19	20	21	22	23	24	25
26	27	28	29	30	31	

Alice and Ellen Kessler
Sandra Milo
Stefania Sandrelli

1964

Raffaella Carrà
Luciana Paluzzi

1966

Luciana Paluzzi

NOVEMBER 1970

S	M	T	W	T	F	S		S	M	T	W	T	F	S
1	2	3	4	5	6	7		22	23	24	25	26	27	28
8	9	10	11	12	13	14		29	30					
15	16	17	18	19	20	21								

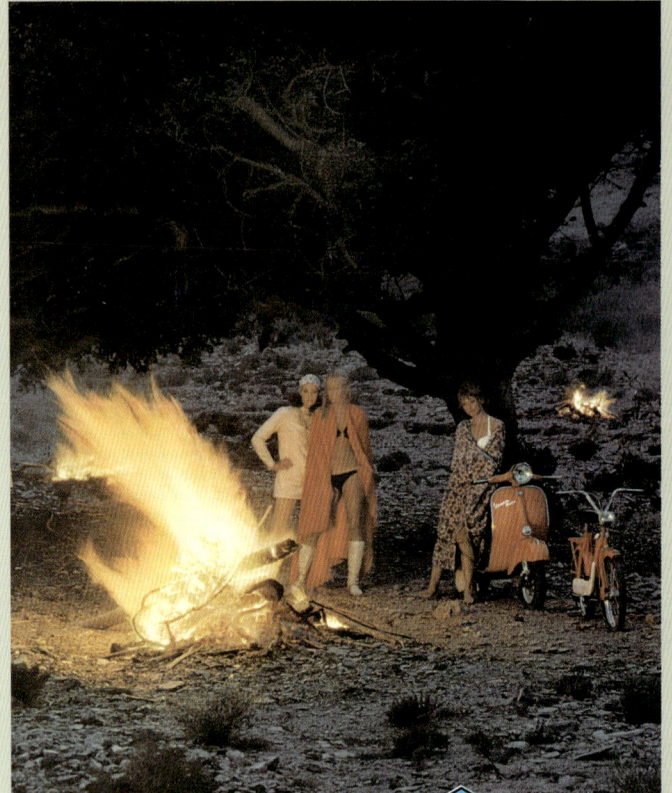

DECEMBER 1970

S	M	T	W	T	F	S		S	M	T	W	T	F	S
		1	2	3	4	5		20	21	22	23	24	25	26
6	7	8	9	10	11	12		27	28	29	30	31		
13	14	15	16	17	18	19								

1970

1989

Viaggiate

Frames from a life-long movie

Marino Livolsi

There is no industrial object so present in our image of Italians as the **Vespa**. No object provokes memories and emotions as does this "silver thing". Only the car "Seicento" is as present, but has lasted less in time, and has been more of a cultural symbol (the Italy that travels and knows more beyond the closed walls of a house or the few streets of a village or town) than something which truly relates to a moment in the life of most Italians. The **Vespa**, on the contrary, has been possessed, driven, touched and envied by practically everyone who lived in the fifties and sixties.

If we consider this image as a subjective, almost passionate story of something which has lived amidst the life of a person (or social group), then we can see it as expressing itself in our memories as a series of frames. Each one of these reminds us of some event directly experienced or seen running along that ideal stage in which society was represented in those years. Others come directly from the screen, big and small (or from the pages) of the media which, for a certain time, represented a parallel reality, a likely one if not the true one, but one which knew how to create and present scenes and characters which, over time, seem to be real or really existed.

Let's begin looking at some of these frames.

In the first we can see a man and a woman. He is young but not too young, "correctly" dressed, wearing a jacket, a white shirt with the top button undone and no tie. He has black, well combed brillantined hair. She is wearing an elegant dress "for going out", which was almost certainly "homemade" (by herself or by the grisette living on the floor below), she is wearing a very wide skirt, a modest sign of wealth, she sits side-saddle, with both legs on one side of the vehicle. This could not be otherwise, the skirt would not allow it: it would show her legs, an unbearable scandal for those years: her embracing the rider is justifiable for security reasons, even if it still looks a little daring, although it is assumed - within the morality of the times - that the man is the husband or the "official" fiancée and has already been intrduced to, and is now a part of, the family in her home. Certainly the woman doesn't have any pairs of trousers in her wardrobe (unless they are for work) and she would never wear them for going out. Her face possesses the tranquil insouciant beauty characteristic of Italian women of that time. She is very far from the image of the shapely model, although her form would not be described as slim for if she lived today she would definitely consider going on a diet.

He and She together give the sensation of serenity. Some years later on, a government party could have used them to promote the image of "peaceful strength". What, however, immediately comes across, though, is a common obligation to work. This is certainly their fate, even if in her dreams lives the hope of staying at home, looking after her children, and keeping her flat (still most likely rented - for some more years) tidy as best she can. The dream of both is to live better than people did in the recent past, but the fantasy of consumer products, unthinkable for those times, has still not arrived. He and She are riding along the streets of a city (we can see tramlines): they are probably going to visit relatives, or maybe are going to the cinema. It makes us think of a holiday, a day off; cinema in the afternoon, after the morning mass and a bigger lunch than usual.

It is the Italy that is overcoming the difficulties of the post-war years, defeat and great poverty. It is the image of a reconquered serenity: it could be the frame that follows the one where rubble and sad, tense faces appear together. Maybe this Italy has just "passata à nuttata" (passed through the night), as Edoardo put it in his unforgettable metaphor, thus encouraging the desire to turn over a new page and look towards the future and forget the past. So, it is, even if He and She on their **Vespa** have just come from a modest house with little furniture and still less clothes in the wardrobe, it looks as though they are heading towards a brighter future where they will be able to realise many of their dreams. For this reason they have smiles on their faces, as if to say these are still hard times, but that something is changing for the better. We can picture the photograph that immediately follows, where two extraordinary domestic appliances appear: a refrigerator and a television being carried into their house.

But let us not anticipate the rest of the story. If the photo were the picture frame of a film we would see other things of great interest. Especially the anonymously constructed houses of the city and shops with modest signs and little merchandise in their windows. Many people on foot and very few motorcars on the road. The outskirts of the town immediately merging into the countryside: the tram terminus is surrounded by green, and many use this service to take a trip "fuori porta" (outside the city gates), travelling with food prepared at home until they reach humble inns, where it is possible to have food which the war made disappear from shop counters. The roads still need to be asphalted. And the odd motorcycle or horse and cart pass along them. Few houses of modest appearance block the expanse of fields. Missing are the small factories and billboards along the sides of the roads, yet to come.

If with a quick flashback we go back to the city, we can see that the many people crowding the pavements look very like our two protagonists in the photo. They are not dressed too expensively, rather modestly, actually, even if they try - with all their might - to be up to standard. A few men are wearing hats. Hardly anyone is carrying a bag: paper bags of the consumer era are still unknown. The thing we notice most of all is the difficulty in distinguishing among different ages: old people and children aside, they all seem to be about thirty years old. Maybe because they are dressed more or less in the same way and seem to have similiar faces. Only along the streets of the centre of town can we see more elegance, but even here there is a certain uniformity to it. Maybe this is because everyone - especially the women - are very natural looking in aspect. There is no sophistication: the women are wearing very little makeup. Their dresses and hair styles are grisette versions of dress pattern models or in imitation of the stars of the cinema screen. Very few people in the classy quarters are wearing clothes from the large fashion houses. The middle classes, the "petite bourgeoisie", seem to occupy the streets of the city. The higher classes - the rich - live apart and do not let themselves be captured by photographers. At the most they appear on special occasions: for example in magnificent pomp at the inauguration of the opera season. Women spend most of their time at home. The workers live in the suburbs outside town and are hardly ever seen on the streets, or mentioned in the newspapers. Only at specific times of the day, but only in certain areas of the city, can we see them entering or leaving the factory gates in swarms. Some on bicycles, others on mopeds. It is not by chance that in a famous **Vespa** advertisement - this time a drawing - we can see a strong, but smartly dressed worker on his **Vespa** going (and exuding a smug sense of security as he goes) to his place of work, while other people in the background - at the edges of this caricature - are running there on foot or towards an overflowing tram, impossible to board, heading for the same place.

And so our journey to a past era still far away - and not because of the years that separate us - is concluded. Perhaps our man on the **Vespa** is the same one, even if captured in

per il vostro lavoro
per il vostro svago

Vespizzatevi

Italian society, still closely linked to its rural background, in a famous advertisement of the 50's: "Vespizzatevi!" ("Vespa yourselves!")

two different moments. In the photograph he is with his wife on a festive holiday; in the drawing he is alone while riding to work. He is the same anonymous Italian pursuing the dreams of all his compatriots on the journey which will lead his country towards the economic boom. Slowly as the years go by, his (though be they modest) dreams start taking form: having more money to buy what he has never been able to have and which, now are beginning to appear in the shop windows: electrical appliances and other household "things", clothes, cars with low cylinder engines. But the change is more profound, and has not come about merely through the acquisition of consumer products, even if they give meaning to and promote the spirit of the times. For example, for young people the moment has arrived where they are no longer victims of social forms of impediments. Now it is easier for boys to meet girls, they are not expected as much to bow down to their superiors, new rites and myths are beginning: they can now go out in groups and "hang out" on the streets or in bars, not only in church halls or youth clubs as they could only do before. Our country is collectively celebrating a sort of initiation towards modernity, a moving away from provincialism. Now it is young men who are different from their fathers and hope for different things for their own children. It is a modest but almost obstacle-free climbing up of the social ladder: every year people are better off than the previous one and they hope, with reasonable optimism, that they will be even more better off the year after that. It is a change that is going through individuals and then through society itself. In fact, it is not a cultural or moral change as such. Everything has taken place very quickly and almost by chance. People leave the country for the city, travel up from the South to the North, change their jobs. But all this is "their own business". No help is given, there are no exemplars to be followed, except those of their own relatives or friends. For some the adventure results in a swift bettering of their ways, while others expend more time and fatigue on it. Others end up on the roadside. It is the Italy Visconti narrated in *Rocco e i suoi fratelli* (Rocco and his brothers). Everything is changing so quickly that there is just no time to stop and try to understand or meditate on what is happening. It is more with amazement than pleasure that we read the story in the newspapers informing us that a miracle has taken place: "there are no more poor people!". But not everybody knows or is aware of this: especially when this news comes straight after heavy winds of recession and political instability thus making us fear that it is all an illusion.

Italy and Italians are always the same: the changes that take place do so within tradition and in the family. An Italian is more concerned about what is happening around him than what is happening nationally.

And it is for this reason that the world of consumer products, coming within our domestic walls, is so important and full of meaning. Television puts us in contact with the rest of the world, the refrigerator presents us with diverse ways of attending to family needs and planning our food purchases. But it is, above all, the **Vespa** that, over these years - may we call it the busy hornet? ("vespa" means wasp in Italian) - has taken people to places never seen before, or has given them the opportunity to do things (either at work or in their free time) never done before. It is the **Vespa** that has become the standard bearer of these exemplary products, riding along with them and keeping close to the demands of the period. It is worth noting, however, that the slightest change the **Vespa** undergoes over, say, a few years, is a significant one. At first it is greenish and not wondrously beautiful: a symbol of the transformation from reconverted industries to the fight for peace. Then it beco-

**Opposite:
"Vespizzatevi!"
("Vespa
yourselves!"):
the slogan
winks together
with Tina Pica
in *Mia nonna
poliziotto* ("My
grandma the
policewoman")**

mes white and elegant; one of the products that imposes the "stile italiano" (Italian style) onto the world. It is its tranformation through time from necessity to elegance and its mysterious recipe of "the good life" which amazes the whole world. It is not by chance that **Vespa** is also "la Dolce Vita" appearing as it does in Fellini's film as the image which makes foreigners look upon Italy with amazement and admiration. And then the **Vespa** is dressed in silver and becomes beautiful, a myth of elegance, youth and of all possible adventures. With the "Vespone" (big wasp) we give ourselves wings and let our hair down: What is now noise and vulgarity was then a sort of liberation rite. The young man riding it is a modern Prince Charming: the fiancée that every girl would like to have; or he's the exciting "latin lover" who drives legions of female tourists from the North on the beaches of Emilia Romagna. The **Vespa**, indefatigable and invincible, rides out from the confines of its country and invades the roads of the world: it zips around Paris, London, Madrid and the countries of the North. It is Italy's messenger: hailing a country which is backward no longer, but is rather genial for the things it has created and designed. Adventurous it is too: to the North Pole it goes, trips around the world it makes and upon strange rafts it sails the seas.

Surrounding the **Vespa** are all the symbols of desire; the pretty young fiancées, precocious girls - advertising for calendars - (yet to become sophisticated models), stage and film stars posing for photographers. It represents the thrill of society life or "sins" of which nowadays could even concern someone who, at that time, was totally excluded, someone who didn't even think that certain things existed or could happen at all.

It is the celebration of a myth, of a season which ends, as in all fairy tales, with the story of a romantic princess and a seductive journalist who in *Vacanze Romane* (a famous film with Gregory Peck and Audrey Hepburn) discover "Love" and a fantastic city, on their **Vespa**. It is the dream tale narrated for grown-ups: the **Vespa** permits anything, and rides with us along the most important moments of our lives. The sweet smile of a much loved actress, and the charm of a great and much loved and famous actor - this is the projection of love, carried far away by the **Vespa** from the eyes of censors and the curious; and the projection of many adventures (dreamed or realized) along the roads of Italy and Europe. It is the frame of the grand finale of a season in which He and She can arrive somewhere beautiful "mounted upon" their **Vespa**. If *Vacanze Romane* is our popular myth, then the painting by Renato Guttuso (in which two tightly embraced lovers are fleeing away from a difficult situation) is the consecration of it at the highest level of culture of the time.

It is the conclusion of a season that has seen the **Vespa** accompanying and symbolizing the first great turning point of the country during these post-war years. But this myth runs the risk of hiding the new and diverse times in which the necessity of mass production and, consequently, an efficient marketing and communications policy, pose diverse objectives. More models with more powerful cylinder engines must be designed to satisfy different wants. New markets have been sought into existence. And at this point we feel it is opportune to mention the **Vespa**'s working sister (the Ape - this means bee in Italian and is a small truck on wheels). In many cases (e.g. small business artisans in the south) the Ape is the symbol of the small but innovative entrepreneur. It is a vehicle which can go everywhere, which can climb up steep mountain roads, which can carry a ton load of goods, which is able to cope with complicated deliveries etc...

Now we come to the second great chapter of the story of the **Vespa**. This begins with

**Opposite:
Alessandra
Panaro during
the "Miss
Lazio" beauty
contest
in 1955**

110

a series of foresights to what will happen later on. Above all, the emergence of ecology as a scientific study: a famous campaign ("Sardomobili", a funny "mixture" of sardines and cars) brought to notice the problems of traffic and pollution long before all this became recognisable and serious to society. On the whole, though, the **Vespa** has always been associated with green, it speaks of freedom and large spaces: it almost seems to be the unheard voice for a "compatible" (as it would be defined today) development of less degraded urban spaces.

These foresights, though, are the product of a great publicity launch. Today the great **Vespa** advertising campaigns seem normal or are a historical inventory; but it is enough to remember the slogan: "Chi **Vespa** mangia le mele" ("Who **Vespas** eats the apples") to credit Piaggio with great merit of innovation in the history of advertising. Piaggio have always had touches of originality in their publicity: take for example their slogan: "Vespizzatevi!" ("Vesparise yourselves!") during the initial post-war years; which seemed to mimic other campaigns (or injunctions) which were in the style of the nineteen twenties. And it is a little paradoxical that it was this slogan that had the most success.

The "Chi Vespa" campaign may well have been the watershed in Italian advertising history. The step forward made was the clever use of "motivation research" (so termed at the time) conducted by highly esteemed experts. And what courage of invention; which hitherto Italian advertising campaigns were lacking in! Piaggio's assault and surreal sounding "Chi mangia le mele...e chi no!..." ("He who eats the apples... and he who doesn't!") upon the senses of a still rather provincial public unaccustomed to the "grand buffet" advertising of the eighties, was a calculated risk but nevertheless an act of courage. Success was immediate: everybody spoke of it, attempting to interpret its cryptic message and coming up with differing and outlandish interpretations. Then, for a certain period of time, variations on the theme were created. The base being a household catchphrase repeated: who "does a certain thing"... "eats the apple"..., who "doesn't"... "doesn't"... The broadness of the message, lying between the surreal and the unconscious, showed that Piaggio knew how to convince and involve a very wide public. The invention is almost genial: the **Vespa** as an apple: full of its tasty fruit and object of temptation and desire. The identification is explicit: "a bite on the apple and... a *vroom* on the **Vespa**...".

There are two features of this campaign which were little considered at the time, but that now I feel essential for appraisal. The first is the consequences of the slogan "...lasciati indietro tutti quelli senza fantasia" ("leave behind all those without fantasy"). The second regards the actors or subjects who appear in various versions of Piaggio's commercials: these characters are always young people, often couples, or in groups. Today it is easy to say that all this presaged another great turning point of Italian culture: the discovery of the world of the young and their culture. Youths first "On the Road" and in small cohesive groups, and then, en masse, in contestation. The **Vespa** ads seem to foresee certain themes: freedom (sexual and otherwise), "being together", but above all, refusal of traditional culture. The culture that has always existed; which had known how to create the economic boom, but without coming off the rails grounded by tradition and the family; a culture incapable of inventing different ways of living or thinking. Leaving behind "all those without fantasy" seems almost a battle cry, an incite to change, a rejection of all and everything that stands for the past.

Having fantasy and understanding the world that is changing; the new opportunities that a society can offer when it is unbound by poverty and released from the rigidity of power from leaders who "counted". Having the imagination to plan one's life as one wants, with the person one loves, and where one wants, doing things that one feels are pleasing and important to do. And so, here we are, for a brief moment, with the apparition of the Italian dream, of a healthy industrial society, without problems or contradictions.

And it is not by chance that it has been in these years that **Vespa** has come up with a new product with this particular "target" in mind: the Ciao (this is a type of moped). Having been defined and analysed by research teams this "target" is young people, also the very young, teenagers still at school, all with a strong propensity to be part of a group, attentive to new fashions and the lingo of youth sub-culture. But there is a little surprise: a part of this "target" is composed of young girls who are not in the least embarrassed about enjoying this product (up until this point it was only a man or a boy who drove a **Vespa**) for going out, meeting up with friends, openly being with, and not having to hide their boyfriends, etc... In the marketing of Piaggio and in the culture of the country, the signs of change are all there: an alternative culture, new lifestyles (in which certain consumer goods will always play an important role), the nascent waves of feminism. The "Vespino" (little wasp) and the Ciao preside over this period, just as the **Vespa** rode along with the liberation (first economic then cultural) of the young people of "'68" from their parents. It is worth noting that the "motorini" (mopeds) are not represented as the image of the more extremist antiestablishment groups which attempt the use of violence for their cause. Here within the collective image of this period there are high cylinder motorbikes and cars: it is these vehicles that remember this "frame" together with arms and mountain passes. And so this is almost an apologue, after twenty-five years, a "splendido quarantenne" (good looking man in his forties) who declares to be a son of "'68", rides around the streets of Rome on his **Vespa**, thinking over his life and everything that has happened to him in that (apparently unmoved) city during those convulsive, and not always bright years. The Vespa seems as though it has been resuscitated from a deceptively far away epoch which is actually very near. It could almost be said that no other Piaggio product has had the same symbolic connotations as **Vespa** simply because the country did not want it, being busy with, first, overcoming the "anni di piombo" (the years of lead: referring to the heavy years of violent terrorist acts) and then the squandering of money and time on an obsessive infatuation with consumer goods.

It is obvious that that is not how it stands. The history of Piaggio could provide us with other motives and causes. But the reasons why the car has definitively superseded the "motorino", why ecological illusions of development without urban chaos and pollution are complex and mysterious, cannot be explained merely by the affirmation of an industrial sector or company. Certainly, the new **Vespa** which came out in the seventies, could not have modified the history of this country. It is evocative, though, to think that certain hopes have faded together with the symbol of two great cultural turning points which Italy has lived through with great ardour. A coincidence indeed, but also a possible way of viewing the social involvement of Italians regarding the apparently only frivolous side of their desires for products which, at times, knew how to evoke themes and emotions unconnected to the functions for which they were created.

Outside they're working on revolution...
Gilberto Filippetti

At the "Disegnando **Vespa**" (Drawing the Vespa) exhibition (Rome, July 1996), a friend of mine who wanted to pay me a compliment said to me, "You know, I think that campaign of yours has turned into a kind of evergreen in our feelings: like certain songs, or the hairstyle that boys had in that period, or like the "angeli del ciclostile" (duplicator angels) that whizzed around on their **Vespas** from one faculty to another, where they got up on to the benches and slammed the obtuse incapacity of adults to understand our new thirst for freshness. Just the memory of it is enough to bring back all the energy, and the struggles, which may have been Utopian, but were undoubtedly happy. We were lucky enough to be twenty when twenty-year-olds were in fashion. It doesn't happen to everybody!" After comments more or less like this, my friend added, "When we've got the time, tell me how the idea came to you."

As in every age, in that period there were people who were twenty years old, and others who weren't. But for the first time, only people who were *really* twenty counted. I remember that period as one fantastic party, so brilliant and exciting that it was impossible not to tremble at the thought that it might break out into hysteria. A party, though, that had its programme. And a wonderful one: imagination, happiness, sexuality and youth in power. Before turning into a political struggle, "that period" had started as a joyful clash between generations. We had immediately defined it as "the revolution of joy". Young people were watched, studied, copied and envied by the "grigi" (grey-haired ones), and besides their arrogance at feeling they were the protagonists of an unrepeatable moment of vitality and creativeness, they boldly challenged the incapacity of adults to understand their new demands. They had even invented a language of their own so as to be even more incomprehensible to the "grey ones", who slipped away, escaping from the squares where the "long-haired yobs" pulled the road up amid the squealing of jeep tyres.

The Beatles, Rubin, Cleaver, Ginzberg, Warhol: an overwhelming flood of stimuli, of thought, of images, of music and poetry, all together and all brand-new. A shock-wave, a colossal big bang! But the chance of a lifetime for a country lad like me (from Iesi, in the Marche region), who had just arrived in Florence, and was only a bit older than the twenty-year-olds. How satisfying it was to let *your* youth and freshness find its place in the demand for youth and freshness. You only needed to look around to appreciate the depth of that moment, to feel an overwhelming sense of being contemporary, to understand that everything that had happened in the past had only been a preparation for that magical period that you were now living. You had to bite into that moment, and join in the party, because you could feel that everything that came after it would only be a clumsy attempt to prolong that brand-new happiness: twenty years old like never before.

That day, I was returning to the office after the lunch break, drenched in the flood of stimuli that rained on me from all sides. I was looking out of the bus window, thinking about the new **Vespa** campaign that I was working on. The bus suddenly braked, and someone said, "There they are again! The usual procession of bloody-minded students!". The first sticks of explosive could be heard whistling through the air, and the police sirens and jeeps were arriving. Sitting inside the bus, protected from the smoke outside, I watched from a window. Completely ignoring all the chaos around him, with an apple between his teeth, he was calmly, impassively, painting on the wall in big white letters: "Don't trust anyone over thirty". Cataclysmic. A new commandment, never heard before. Words used like a weapon, which swept away half the people on board the bus, and left me with the feeling that an idea like that, and words like that, would open up an epoch of passion.

A new idea suddenly makes you grow older, and even if I wasn't so far on in years, I instantly felt decrepit. When he had finished painting his message, the boy turned his lucid, intelligent eyes challengingly towards us. At that time, eyes were the real status symbol. If you're twenty, you're in, I thought, if you're thirty, you're not, and a bit frustrated, I added: "You're working on the revolution, I'm working on **Vespa**!". Back at the office, I stared at the blank sheet of paper in front of me, reflecting on those words, and the idea. It would be nice to try and interpret this new reality for **Vespa**, in the language that was born from it. The ability to understand change as it is taking place, and to tune in to the wave-length of reality and information is a gift that either you've got or you haven't, I told myself, sophisms don't exist. Thinking of the boy, I felt I could do it; it would be enough to trace back every hypothesis for the presentation of **Vespa** to the roots of expression that lay at the basis of that behaviour. I meditated on the force of those words, which created a clear gap between two areas of belonging, pushing two cultures to come to grips with each other and fight. A generation war, joy vs. boredom. All good concepts, but I continued to see, on the blank sheet of paper, the same metallised-grey **Vespa** of the black-and-white films in front of me. Or else the autarchic little car-like **Vespa** of workers who commuted to and from work, stuffing the "L'Unità" newspaper between their pullover and their chest to protect themselves from the cold. And then there were the suggestions of the marketing office, to make things worse. I never used to give them a glance, but this time ... A) Sixteen million young people desire to become mobile; B) Extra-family integration; C) Self-affirmation; D) Post-adolescence frustration; E) Time-saving; F) Need for diversion and "leisure". I swear it, that was exactly what it said: "leisure". In the meantime, outside, that boy was continuing to paint out his new message, to rejuvenate society and free it from idiotic expressions like these, as he angrily bit into his apple.

Berkeley, Paris, Pisa, Trento and Turin had simultaneously caught fire, and were ringing their bells and flashing like slot machines that had hit the jackpot. And in half the countries of the world, other word-weapons were dripping in white paint down the walls of the villas of the "grey ones" and of the "chi no" (those who "don't"): "We want everything and we want it now!", "Don't waste life simply earning a living!", "Throw the greasy meatball away!", "Freedom means not having anything to lose!", "Love is to be shared like bread!", "Black is beautiful!", "Woman is beautiful!", "Young is beautiful!" for all the Sino-Afro-Yugo-Andalusian boys. OK, then, let's get it up to top speed: rev up your pen, and leave all that marketing devoid of imagination behind! Five or six words like those for **Vespa**, now, the joy of a campaign to forget old-style dirges like "Digestivo Antonetto", and to bring up to date that icy form of communication like Olivetti's. On with the slang of feelings, light and warm. If you're young, you think cheerfully, and so I wrote on the board, that had turned into a wall: "He who **Vespas** does, he who doesn't, doesn't." The pen was writing by itself: variant A: "He who **Vespas** touches the sun, he who doesn't **Vespa** doesn't". Variant B, "He who **Vespas** eats the apple, he who doesn't, doesn't". That's it! Eureka! Yes, that boy would have painted up a sentence like that. As simple as that. I rang Pico (Tamburini, the head of the Leader company), and he answered "Great, Gib! As fresh as rain-water! It'll be a devil of a job to sell it, though". I could already imagi-

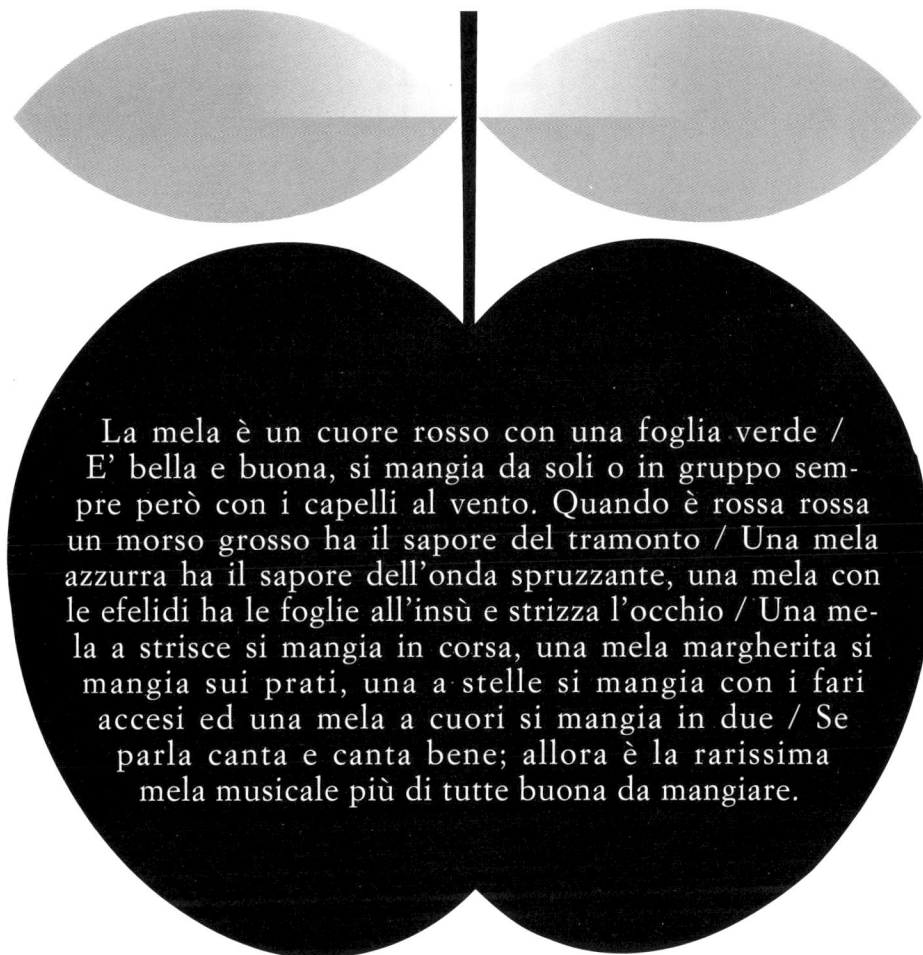

La mela è un cuore rosso con una foglia verde /
E' bella e buona, si mangia da soli o in gruppo sempre però con i capelli al vento. Quando è rossa rossa
un morso grosso ha il sapore del tramonto / Una mela
azzurra ha il sapore dell'onda spruzzante, una mela con
le efelidi ha le foglie all'insù e strizza l'occhio / Una mela a strisce si mangia in corsa, una mela margherita si
mangia sui prati, una a stelle si mangia con i fari
accesi ed una mela a cuori si mangia in due / Se
parla canta e canta bene; allora è la rarissima
mela musicale più di tutte buona da mangiare.

ne the "don't" members of the apparatus clashing with the "do's" at the presentation meeting, and their questions and answers: "But why an apple?", "Transgression and freshness,
sir", "But we sell **Vespas**!", "So good that you could eat them, sir", "But what about this
strange slogan?" "We're selling to eighteen-year-olds, sir". And the nastiest of all (a true a-
necdote): "Who's financing this, the local farm consortium? Come on, Professor Zancani,
call up Filippetti at the Leader office, and ask him at least to adjust the grammar. Put in a nice verb after the noun, and make it sound sweeter, it'll be less traumatic!" , "If I understand
what you mean, sir, rather than "Rome or death", you would prefer "Civitavecchia and se-
riously wounded?". Dr. Zancani, who at the time was Manager of the Advertising Office in
Genoa, immediately welcomed the idea of that screwy campaign, and like the true child of
the 1968 revolution that he was, he succeeded in getting it accepted by the Top Management. The tests carried out said that it was an "extremely dangerous idea", but he decided
that Piaggio was going to make a contribution to the revolution of joy, and this was a way
for the company to share with young people in bringing imagination to power. And conse-

quently: "The apple is a red heart with a green leaf / it's eaten alone or in company, but always with your hair streaming in the wind / A ripe apple is to be eaten at sunset / A blue apple is to be eaten on the rocks / A starry apple is to be eaten with your headlights on / Just bite the apple, rev up your **Vespa** and leave all those people devoid of imagination behind you". Who knows, perhaps that boy would have found them a bit too poetic... Full steam ahead, with freedom, with a syntax that had become congested in its urgent desire to be renewed, and finally with enthusiasm, accelerating in order to derive the visual from the synergic experience of the words, with a clear perception of belonging to one's own time. The words burst the banks of habit by themselves, in an attempt to recover a phonic vitality that has been dampened by the rules of syntax. Like that boy, I too had taken it into my head that day to collaborate in changing those few inches of the world that everybody, at least once in his life, is called to change. Because if you don't do it, you've always lived inside a wardrobe. Six months later, with a barrage of fire never used before by Piaggio, "Who **Vespas** eats the apple, he who doesn't, doesn't" and the apple with two bites taken out of it penetrated into the pages and through the walls of houses in double-page advertisements in all the magazines, on posters, at Esso stations, on TV, on T-shirts sold at UPIM, and on an infinite series of gadgets. All kinds of comments were made, but people immediately spoke of a "campaign-event". "He who **Vespas**" entered into the collective imagination. Dario Fo used it as a basis for a song of political satire which he sang at the *Festival dell'Unità*, Crepax made his famous character say, "Valentina people eats the apple", Umberto Eco commented on the semantic contents of the campaign in the magazine "Espresso", the verb "vespare" (to **Vespa**) ended up in the Zingarelli dictionary, the magazine "Millimetro" came out with a cover-page dedicated to the apple, and the title "An apple and a strange verb overturn creativeness", the magazine "Capitale" quoted "Who **Vespas**" as one of the five most creative campaigns in the last ten years, and an opinion poll defined it as the "best remembered campaign in the last 30 years". Nobody realised, however, and this is the first time that I am revealing it, that when I designed that apple, I was also attempting an experiment that was quite new for that period: a subliminal portrait of the **Vespa**, in which the fruit was the shield and the leaves were the handle-bars. The first campaign that I did for **Vespa** is like the first **Vespa** that you own; it makes you prouder than any other car you may have afterwards.

I went on working with **Vespa** for another sixteen years, creating new campaigns, and **Vespa** repaid me by forcing me to keep up with everything that was changing around me, making me live more in harmony with my time. Then she overtook me, and went on ahead, becoming a myth. But the two of us know, even if we don't tell anyone, that a part of that myth stems from the impression made by those campaigns of mine. She used them every time to become young again.

Every now and then, I wonder what may have come of that boy who painted words on the walls, using them as weapons. Has he, too, by now become a member of the "those who don't"? I imagine him still going around on his **Vespa**, at a good speed, so as not to reveal to anybody that the secret of his eternal youth is "Who **Vespas** does".

... but I'm working on Vespa

Gilberto Filippetti, the creative art director of the Leader agency, gives exemplary expression to the new demands arising from the world of young people. From the late 60's to the early 80's, Vespa advertising follows the course of public criticism, and the growing new awareness of the environment. The problems of young people and Women's Lib enter into the history of communication through Vespa advertising.

1968

chi "Vespa" mangia

(chi non "

PIAGGIO

e mele

spa"no)

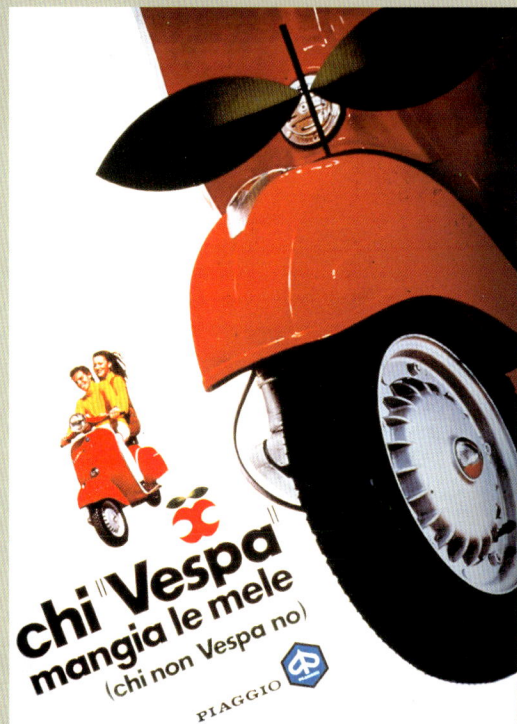

chi "Vespa"
mangia le mele
(chi non Vespa no)
PIAGGIO

1969

chi "Vespa" mangia le mele
(chi non Vespa no)
PIAGGIO

chi "Vespa" mangia le mele

1969

perchè la mela? perchè:
per me è romantica
per me è "spaziale"
somiglia a un bacio
per me ha fatto moda
la "Vespa" naturalmente
chi "Vespa" mangia le mele
(chi non Vespa no)
PIAGGIO

chi "Vespa" mangia le mele
(chi non Vespa no)
PIAGGIO

chi "Vespa" mangia le mele
PIAGGIO

1970

a chi gli pare

PIAGGIO

Operazione '71
melacompro
la Vespa!

PIAGGIO
convince
con la gamma due ruote
unica al mondo
Vespa·Gilera·Ciao·Boxer

1970/ 1971

le sardomobili
non godono il sole

splende "chi Vespa"

PIAGGIO cambia il mondo in 2 ruote

le sardomobili
si rubano l'aria

respira "chi Vespa"

PIAGGIO cambia il mondo in 2 ruote

1972

le sardomobili
si sfidano sempre

pace "chi Vespa"

PIAGGIO cambia il mondo in 2 ruote

le sardomobili
non amano gli altri

rispetta "chi Vespa"

PIAGGIO cambia il mondo in 2 ruote

1972

le sardomobili
urlano a clacson

sussurra 'chi Vespa'

le sardomobili hanno 4 ruote: ma vorrebbero averne 2 come la Vespa. È Vespa: oggi più di sempre, è il mezzo più giovane e attuale perché è pulita di fuori e di dentro. Dici anche tu "metacompro la Vespa" e lasciati indietro tutti quelli senza fantasia. Vespa: 7 modelli con prestazioni e motori diversi.

PIAGGIO cambia il mondo in 2 ruote

1972

le sardomobili
si rubano il tempo

**fa prima
"chi Vespa"**

🔷 **PIAGGIO** cambia il mondo in 2 ruote

Vespa: muove la voglia di fare.

PIAGGIO

voglia di concretizzare le idee

Vespa: muove la voglia di fare.

PIAGGIO cambia il mondo in 2 ruote

1974

Vespa dà una svolta alle cose

ci sono un sacco di cose che vale la pena di fare

Vespa: dà una svolta alle cose

Piaggio cambia il mondo in 2 ruote

PIAGGIO

1975

Un giorno un piccolo aereo lasciò le ali in cielo per diventare un mito in terra.

Era il giorno
di una intuizione perfetta, fatta per durare.
Era una idea circondata da piccole, misteriose
leggende, che la volevano figlia dell'aria,
scesa dal cielo per correre leggera,
sicura della sua nobile origine aeronautica.
Così Vespa abbandonò le ali per vestirsi di una
forma d'acciaio diventata grande nei nostri cuori.
Vespa figlia dell'aria.

Vespa, il mito scooter.

PIAGGIO

1976

Gennaio, febbraio, Marx, aprile… i ragazzi diventano uomini e Vespa cresce con loro.

Vespa, il mito scooter.

PIAGGIO

Che quel giorno fu un grande giorno lo disse anche il Museo d'Arte Moderna di New York.

Quel giorno,
in una mostra dedicata al Design Industriale,
il Museo d'Arte moderna di New York
classificò la Vespa fra i migliori prodotti industriali
realizzati in serie, per il suo styling purissimo
che raccontava al mondo intero il talento del Made in Italy.
Così Vespa entra nell'arte con la bellezza italiana
ed un nome che suona di composta e pulita leggerezza.
Vespa figlia dell'arte.

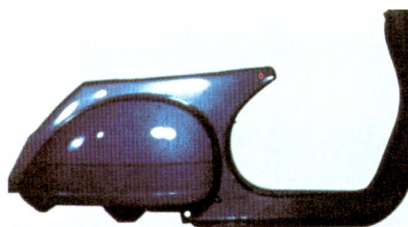

Vespa, il mito scooter.

PIAGGIO

Come ci muoveremo nel futuro si legge meglio sulle strade che in cielo.

Vespa, il mito scooter.

PIAGGIO

1976

Oggi sono la frontiera.

la tua Vespa, chiedila agli "Uomini Azzurri"
4 modelli PK - 3 modelli PX

PIAGGIO

Oggi sono il bosco.

PIAGGIO

IO V

VESPA, LA T

la tua Vespa chiedila agli
UOMINI AZZURRI

PIAGGIO

1977/ 1978

ESPA, TU JANE
A LIANA DA CITTA'

1981

L'Ita
s'è

NUOVE VESPA PK 50 E 1

lia !

6 / L'ITALIA S'E' VESPA

PIAGGIO

1982

I remember...

I remember that when I was eighteen years old she was thirty. Not my fiancée: my **Vespa**. She, my fiancée, was eighteen like myself. And unfortunately, she didn't have a **Vespa**.

I remember that there was the **Vespa** Primavera known as "*il* Primavera". One hundred and twenty-five c.c., a number plate and no helmet, for then the state and its laws wasn't worried about our health, and so we rode on with the wind in our hair and gnats in our eyes; such delight was ours and the shampoo companies'! Il Primavera was the top in style, like Borroughs shoes and blue raincoats. We could "ride in twos", an expression that immediately brings us back to erotic epiphanies never again experienced. If she loved you, you understood straight away at the first bump: if she planted her nails into the seat so as not to embrace you, she didn't love you: orshe sympathized with Communion and Liberation.

I remember after that came the "cinquantino" (little fifty - referring to the size of the engine). A tiny **Vespa** on which you couldn't ride in twos (we did all the same, though, tight though it was: but comfort wasn't the problem; it was more the having to jump off in flight when we saw the police coming that was annoying. You found yourself stranded on foot in the middle of the road and you never knew what face to make. Parentheses within parentheses: years later I went to Naples and there I discovered that you can ride in threes: I should have been brought up there instead! End of parentheses.) "Il cinquantino"'s top speed was 42 kilometres per hour. This, over all our national territory except Emilia Romagna: in this region, where people fiddled with engines, even with those of electric razors, "il cinquantino" could reach up to 120 and consume as much as a BMW. Where we lived, however, it reached up to 42. Its special feature was an excessive noise which perforated the air driving crazy the old pensioners sitting on their benches: who, on the passing by of our subject in question, would "shoot" filthy words at us; words which would turn a statue pale. The rider, however, couldn't hear them, for being an owner of a 'cinquantino' his hearing had already long gone to pieces.

I remember that towards the end the "Vespone" (big **Vespa**) came out. Only grown-ups had it. It was fat at the hips and it was, in its way, uncannily silent. One day you woke up, discovered you liked it or "him", fat and silent, and then you understood that you had grown up.

I remember that the **Vespa** was started by kickstarting a pedal sticking out of the right side of the motorcycle. It was a pretty innocuous looking pedal: but the truth was it was a really wicked little buggar. One out of ten times it came off the engine and became as limp as a wet sock. You gave it all your weight and the wet sock disconnected firing your foot to the asphalt like an omlette falling from the thirtieth floor. The pain began at the heel until it worked its way up to your head where it blended with the evident feeling of self-mortification at the impression created in front of onlookers. You suffered in silence, but it was real pain, that, I can tell you.

There were four methods of starting it. 1) *Cool.* One acts on the pedal with the left foot, maintaining the body in an upright posture while continuing to chat away with onlookers as if everything were normal. The **Vespa** started one time out of two. 2) *Sportive.* One acts on the pedal, with the right foot which obliges one to bend over towards the **Vespa** while grasping the handlebars and thus assuming a vaguely aerodynamic posture. The **Vespa** started one time out of two. 3) *English.* One sits on the seat and kickstarts the pedal behind while maintaining a fixed, fierce stare ahead. Frequent wrenches in the back. The **Vespa** started one time out of two. 4) *Desperate.* One puts it into second gear, squeezes the clutch and then begins to run, pushing. When the engine naughtily simulates a sign of life, one jumps onto the seat letting off the clutch and a series of impressive bad words. The **Vespa** started one time out of a thousand.

I remember my hands hurting, inevitable for one who rides a **Vespa**. The right hand struggling with the brake lever, evidently designed for the hands of a pianist. The left hand was the real tragedy. The **Vespa** had its gears on the left hand side of the handle bar, which made it look much easier to drive than real motorbikes with their incomprehensible foot-pedal gears. On the **Vespa** you could read them: there were little numbers in red; 1,2,3,4 well imprinted for you to see. And between the first and the second gear a little ball which indicated neutral. On paper "easy-peasy". But manoeuvring that handle was like opening a tin of peaches: either your hand was a pair of pincers or you suffered, and that was that. You "hooked onto" the clutch (that as well, designed for pianists' hands) and then with that lump of iron and rubber in hand your wrist began searching for the right gears, which you found only after having gone through all the others: at the end of the operation you were in pain from your elbow down, as if you had played a set with a pole instead of a racket. However, you were very happy all the same. This I remember well.

I remember my parents preferred the **Vespa** because, they said, it was less dangerous. Maybe they put so much trust into that fairing which protected the legs: from what, it wasn't clear; but it looked safe.

I remember my parents preferred the **Vespa** also because it "dirtied you less": again because of its fairing which at the back hid the engine and its predictable spurts of oil. But this was rendered useless often by the vigorous habit, especially by the most restless, to dismount and throw away the above said fairing, exposing the engine and giving the **Vespa** a more dashing and anarchistic profile. It needs to be said that the **Vespa** with its engine revealed gave a certain prestige to the boys who were riding it, rendering them scientifically more appetizing to girls.

I remember us getting petrol. "Miscela" (a petrol mix), to be precise. There were still those splendid petrol stations with two see-through glass cylinders; the attendant pumped away as if we were at an old oil well in the Far West, the cylinders filled up with a gassy orange juice, the black rubber tube emptied everything into the tank: a ceremony. The **Vespa** had its petrol cap in a genial place: under the seat. You got to the petrol station, put the **Vespa** on its stand and then lifted up the seat. From under there everything spilled out: an anti-theft chain that dirtied the eyes just by looking at it, an indefinte number of rags, tattered dusters, cloths, all perfectly fetid, an old falsely corrected class homework essay, a half attached spring, a hat from a raincoat used during the famous thunderstorm of July '77, an authentically autographed photo of Paolo Pulici (a famous soccer player), a tennis ball, old newspapers and, of course, the circulation booklet, by then illegible. You get to the petrol cap and open it, a sort of archaeological task. When you finally opened it, you glanced down into the tank. Now for this operation you had your specialists: those who knew exactly how much "broth" was still down there. You would see an uncertain sparkling which could mean anything, but they translated it immediately: to the bar and back, no problem. The better ones could work it out without even looking. They shook the **Vespa** a little, and by the sound of distant splashing they could work it out to a tee: it's not enough to get you to school. Maybe they were just throwing out guesses, but believing them was easy, and great fun.

I remember when I was down to reserve. The reserve lever of the **Vespa** was low

**Vespa 50 cc.,
1964 model**

down, in between your legs, between your calves, to be precise. If you turned it to the right you closed the petrol tube. If you turned it to the left you opened the reserve tube. Ending up on reserve was a horrendous sensation. You were riding along smoothly, without the least presage of misadventure, you dribbled around cars and pedestrians, crazy with happiness, then suddenly the engine shut off like the facial expression of a defeatist, it faded into nothingness giving you ten or so metres to save it: ten metres to find that damn lever to give it some oxygen, that is, petrol.

Meanwhile all around you the traffic swallowed you up, you began searching for the lever and felt the sound of the **Vespa** starting under your seat, what you enjoyed was a tiny but enormous tingling sensation: something like the electric happiness you feel when saved from a catastrophe. I know it sounds silly but that was how it was. It is in small things that one is trained to recognise great sensations which are capable of shattering one's life. Cross my heart.

I remember when you rode along the tramlines. There was a strange attraction, almost erotic, between the **Vespas'** wheels, small and feminine, and the tramlines, very serious

and clearly masculine. They sought each other for a long time and finally, as long as you were attentive, they found each other. That was really a strange sensation. The **Vespa** slid away with the libidinous levity of an ice-skater, the prosaic friction with the asphalt disappeared, and what you felt was the absurd sensation of flying. Other times you really did fly, but that sensation was definitely no fun at all!

I remember the speedometer on the "Vespone". Maybe there was also one on the "Primavera", I don't know. But on the "Vespone" there was one, and boy what a one! It always seemed to have a strange feature: for reasons never made clear, when it indicated the speed it did so trembling: for fear, perhaps, or because of some atavistic skepticism regarding any human or mechanical ambitions towards precision, but it trembled nevertheless. And you almost became fond of it when, at the traffic lights, it could have a little rest, finally immobile, on zero. Like Grandpa, who always trembled a little, but stopped when falling into a deep snooze in his armchair, finally happy and immobile.

I remember those who, in winter, put up a "veranda". I mean that kind of plastic windshield that one mounted onto the handlebars and at times even had a little roof to dupe the rain. The more sophisticated also had windscreen wipers. On the whole, though, this was considered "wimpish" or a privilege reserved for adults. But it did work, though: you lost a little speed, of course, but you avoided bronchopneumonia or the newspaper under your pullover.

I remember ladies on the **Vespa** riding side-saddle. Now extremely rare. But this was a masterpiece. Age above 45: he at the handlebars she behind, sitting on one side, with her legs crossed and her gaze, seraphic, lost in admiring the traffic. She would have a handbag somewhere, and add a touch of eroticism with the raise of her skirt. Maybe they had been arguing all day, the two of them, maybe they hated each other, but when you saw them, he at the handlebars and she behind, in that position, you thought they were so "right", so divinely "right" together, that you were moved. And you thought "being in love" must be something like that. Something so "right".

I remember that at a certain point you got it into your head to paint your **Vespa**. Normally this emotional push was due to the repetitive tumbles which had reduced the fairing to a series of colourless chips and scratches. But at other times the impulse was merely exquisitely aesthetic. Pestilential spray-paint cans were sold, not too expensive to deprive you of a little nefariousness. So, you chose a colour (always demented) and you locked yourself in the garage. You covered up all the chrome parts with adhesive tape, and then began to spray. At the end the chrome parts were left inexorably sticky, and the **Vespa** was a sight for sore eyes. More often than not, you sold it.

I remember how "great" it was just sitting on the **Vespa**. When it was standing, I mean. Sitting on the **Vespa** in front of the bar, underneath the fiancée's house, at the school gates, after a football match. Other motorcycles, if you stood them on their stands, were "wonky"; very uncomfortable to sit upon, but the **Vespa** no: perfectly upright. Extremely comfortable. The time spent sitting there was always wasted time. And maybe for this reason in our memory it has been archived as an adorable time, free from misery.

I remember my back light, red: always broken. And the headlight, always a little "cross eyed", in remembrance of its previous tumbles. There were no indicator lights, and one still used that archaic and tiring gesture of extending one's arm to show where the hell one was going. When I saw indicator lights appearing on **Vespas**, I remember understanding that all this was over.

An Indian summer

Antonio Tabucchi

I was between Kancheepuram and Mahabalipuram, in the south of India, where magnificent temples rise. I was travelling in a car driven by an Indian driver, for in India you can't rent cars without drivers, it would be too dangerous. We stopped at a cottage restaurant which was mentioned in the guide book I brought with me, and which, by now, I trusted blindly: "India, A Travel Survival Kit". The cottage was not at all disappointing. It had an ample bamboo terrace, cheered up by large brass air conditioners, where one could have a light breakfast. It was a little past five in the afternoon and the driver and I ordered two teas which were served with biscuits and slices of papaya. I tried to get the driver to tell me about Mahabalipuram, its religious traditions, but he was pretty reticent. Maybe he was simply being discreet, as the Indians are. Probably your guide can give you better information than me, he told me.

I felt far away from everything. This everything being my cultural reference points: the West, my language, European fashions, the company of someone you could really talk to. I decided to continue on my journey again, I wanted to get to Mahabalipuram soon, where there was a hotel waiting that a Goan priest had booked for me, and to discharge that silent and slightly arrogant driver. Anyway, I had promised the hotel in the area I had come from, that the driver would bring the car back that evening. It was appallingly hot.

We got back into the car, a battered vehicle from the sixties. I couldn't tell whether it was American or Japanese. Anyway, what difference did it make? The suspension had already gone and every pothole in the road hit my kidneys. The windows didn't work properly, they only went half way down, and the fake leather seat coverings made my back sweat terribly. I closed my eyes and resigned myself. The road was lined with mango trees, the driver would drive with concentration or smoke one of those little perfumed Indian cigars, made with only one tobacco leaf, that are called "Ganesh". The driver began to smoke, I opened my eyes and looked through the windscreen. We were at a closed level crossing. One can see all sorts of things at level crossings in India. And in fact the travellers standing at the barrier were a mixed bunch. There was a motorised rick-shaw, apparently empty, painted yellow and with an enormous indecipherable sign, probably Hindi, probably in some language of the south. Oh well: the unknown. There was a man standing by his bicycle; his face was tinted with white lead and he had a gauze over his mouth. I was able to understand somewhat what that man was about, he was a believer in the Jainist religion, the white lead was a symbol of humility and the gauze on the mouth prevented him from swallowing an insect, that could be the form of a person who is crossing another plane of existence. There was also an elephant with its forehead painted with violet signs, maybe a sacred elephant, ridden by it's driver. And also there was a man sitting on a scooter. He had two coloured bands around his forehead, a white shirt that came down to his knees, and behind, on his luggage-rack, placed cross-wise, a long and thin covering wrapped with white bands of material that looked like an enormous "baguette".

I asked the driver if he knew what it could be. He sucked on his little cigar and replied peacefully: it's a dead body. I didn't have the courage to ask him again. The sun was now implacable, I was sweating, I felt ill at ease, I wanted to be somewhere else, but I was here waiting at this absurd level crossing, with a motorcyclist carrying a dead body as though it were a postage parcel. I summoned up my strength and asked him again: a dead body, why a dead body? Well, the driver answered phlegmatically, he's probably taking it for bur-

Opposite:
A photo
by Roberto
Patrignani:
a road in New
Delhi, during
the Rome/Tokyo
Vespa rally

ning at a temple in Mahabalipuram, there are pyres at the temples of Mahabalipuram, and the waters of the lakes are holy, and can receive the ashes.

I looked at the motorcyclist through the window. He felt he was being watched and in his turn he looked at me. I smiled at him, he continued to look at me without making a sign. Good morning, I said to him, are you going to Mahabalipuram? The man didn't reply. I would have liked to have asked him something less banal, to have had a brief conversation with him as one does with travellers on the same route, to wish him all the best, maybe, or my condolences. But it was impossible to say any of this to him, simply impossible. And so I said the only thing that came to mind, superfluous information, just silly, and for him, useless. I'm Italian, I told him. He looked at me and his face broadened into a big smile, one of those large very white smiles that Indians from the south have. He gave his scooter a friendly pat, pointed his finger at it and shouted: **Vespa**! And at that moment the train went past, the level crossing barrier went up, my driver drove on, and we left behind the man with his troublesome load. I looked at him from my seat at the back of the car and saw that he was giving me a sign of greeting. And I gave him the thumbs up too, my arm leaning out of the window.

Out to conquer the world

During the 50's and 60's, Vespa flies on the wings of success to all the continents of the world. Soren Nielsen arrives at the Pole (1963), Vespas reach faraway villages in the heart of Africa and the forests of Thailand. Vespa cicle around a bull-ring in Madrid or watch the pitiful performance of a dancing bear in a Balkan village

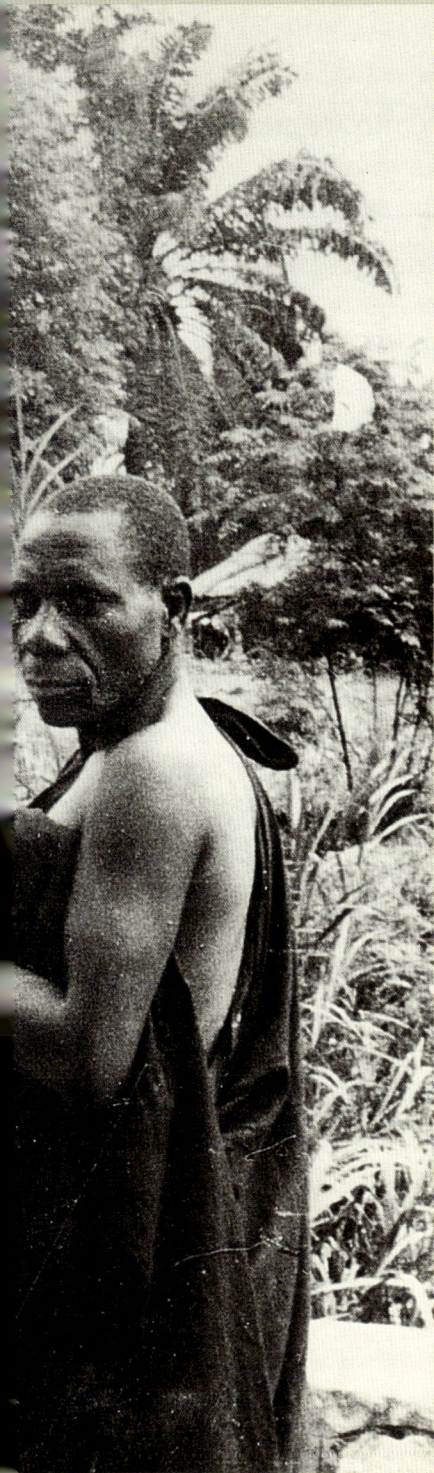

Ciak... on a Vespa!

Lina Wertmuller

Why does an object become a symbol? A question that could set off sociologists and academics, but which in truth is impossible to give an answer to. Of course if we see a traditional scarf for the golf course we think of England, if we see two female legs sheathed in black transparent stockings with a backbround of lace and lacy underwear we think of France. If we see a bull we think of Spain, if we see a big cigar we think of Wall Street... banal, conventional, but it is interesting to reflect on the reasons behind these conventions. It would be too simplistic to reply that golf was born in England; the CanCan in France and bullfighting in Spain. The search should be carried out as to why that game or that dance became conventional "symbols" of a culture. And if Germany has no national symbol - except perhaps some sort of little hat with "Edelweiss" and a mug of beer which could only be exclusively from Baveria - linked to games, dances or forms of entertainment, there must be a reason.

Garrottes, guillotines, gas chambers and other pleasant little objects even though identifying themselves with inquisitions, revolutions, and genocides, haven't ever had to aspire to the ambitious titles of symbols.

In its specific literary meaning a symbol is something which represents something else, with which it is, in some way connected. Alano di Lilla called symbols: emblematic discourses which hide a deeper sense from that which appears. Kant says: the symbol represents a concept indirectly, providing an intuitive image, which indicates "the thought in its effort to represent itself in some sort of symbolised reality". If then we turn to Nietzsche or Freud, the symbol becomes the large protagonist of the mysterious and difficult connection between conciousness and unconciousness, skating dangerously along the edge of an abyss of those unbounded and mysterious labyrinths which philosophy and poetry are. All oneiric images are coded messages which censorship forbids us to receive clearly, isn't that so Doctor Freud? And these messages only via the symbols which ask us for help from the bottom of the black well.

Slowly, slowly as we approach another century, in what is called modern poetry, the symbol is the obscure cipher of a relationship between contingent and absolute things, of which the poet interprets.

Now I do not wish to exaggerate while losing myself in enchanted meanderings and enchanting symbologies, but it is absolutely unquestionable that between psychoanalysis and advertising, we are targets for a machine-gunning of symbols which crowd our day and our life. For this let us turn back to that primitive question: why does an object become a symbol: reply - totally impossible of course, but we must recognise that the popular and universal value of certain things is immediate. My white spectacles, definitive choice for the rest of my life, hiding in their whiteness, the sea air, summer and sun, the joy of life, a counterpoint to the elegant nocturne obscurity of death. The **Vespa** hides an appetitive and merry message in its curves, a perfumed smile of basil and almonds. Yes, let me say it, the old almond, in the game of symbolsm he's there too. The curvaceous breasts and hips of the models of those faraway fifties, sixties so different from the gorgeous but skeletal bisexual top models which today represent female glamour, set fantasy alight. Lollo, Pam Pam and then Sophia Loren, Claudia Cardinale and all that Olympus of fragrant and cordial beauty secretly linked to spaghetti, to the cupolas of the divine baroque churches and to a healthy lust for life, they exuded their secret reference to art, to the optimism of an Italy that was reborn with its beauty and its miseries in a climate of hope and freedom, after so much horror. Perhaps for

Opposite:
Michel Simon

this, apart from Piaggio's skilful advertising campaigns, the **Vespa** was one of the first positive symbols of a reborn Italy, after the war, a symbol of its sunny, beautiful, "simpatica" and vital nature.

Something agile, young, dynamic which straight away identifies itself with the spirit which then animated Italy and which produced the economic boom. Immediately **Vespa** became the symbol and has remained that symbol. I, like many young people of that time, dreamt of having one and in the end my dream came true and I had one.

It was beautiful. We slid around the traffic with ease. We wiggled our beautiful rotund hips as if we were on a pure-bred. Nothing at all to do with those violent and overbearing signs that attached themselves to the motorbike. Those hard metallic symbols of fake strength and of fake revolt, with which the wretched unconciousness of the young often love to hide its own weakness. The **Vespa** smiled, was never threatening. We went on holidays on it and made love on it, there was no arrogance or nastiness. Its proportion was intriguing. It was pleasant and elegant when it went down Via Veneto, it did a spin at the bottom of the steps at Piazza di Spagna, or it took a couple for a trip to Piazza del Popolo. Well, of course, yes, for me the **Vespa** was indissolubly connected to Rome, as it was for young people from Milan, probably connected to Piazza del Duomo o La Scala. Personally I lived with it among baroque churches, fountains, old buildings. And who knows, maybe because of its little aerodynamic curves I always found it in harmony with those classical big clouds of the Roman sky. I'm not suggesting that cherubs or little angels with their pink little bottoms a-seated upon the **Vespa** would have rendered her baroque too, but on the whole, some kinship is there.

The image that fills the Roman and Italian streets in those years and then on and on to today, immediately strikes those eyes attentive to cinema. The **Vespa** had lines and characters, the air of youth and holidays which surrounded it, was immediately identified with it. That one there had what it takes to have a future in cinema.

And so it was that the **Vespa** began her cinematographic career.

No, identifiable means of transport, not even the jeep - protagonist of the Second World War - or the Rolls had such a blinding career in cinema as the **Vespa**. We are talking about around a hundred films. I don't know if I am making myself clear. A true record. And what films! The great Italian directors and many foreign ones. In some cases, as in the celebrated *Vacanze Romane* Audrey Hepburn and Gregory Peck enjoy their adventure to the full around a sunny Rome, riding upon a **Vespa**. That is, the **Vespa** played the role of the protagonist, in many other cases, it was impossible not to have her in films representing roads and Italian piazzas. Those friendly little curves immediately and indissolubly became part of the cinematographic panorama.

The list of those hundred films with their relative directors and actors would be a long one. Of course Fellini, Rosi, De Sica, Rossellini, Antonioni, Monicelli, Pasolini and almost everybody else, including myself also and many others from following generations up to the present day, instinctively ended up by finding her there, on the frame, that diva for whom the years do not go by. Her curves resist fashions, her sprinting still maintains her supremacy in friendliness and practicality. To her all the Japanese waves of those towering black, alarming, enormous and engaging "Samurais" were inferior. Lightness, comfort, the least effort, and "simpatia" made sure that her throne will not be scratched by the whole sea of two wheeled products that have invaded roads and screens in the last ten years. Dra-

Vespa and ancient world: opposite, Mitchell Gordon on the set of one of the many mythological films shot in Rome during the 60's. Above: Charlton Heston on the set of *Ben Hur*

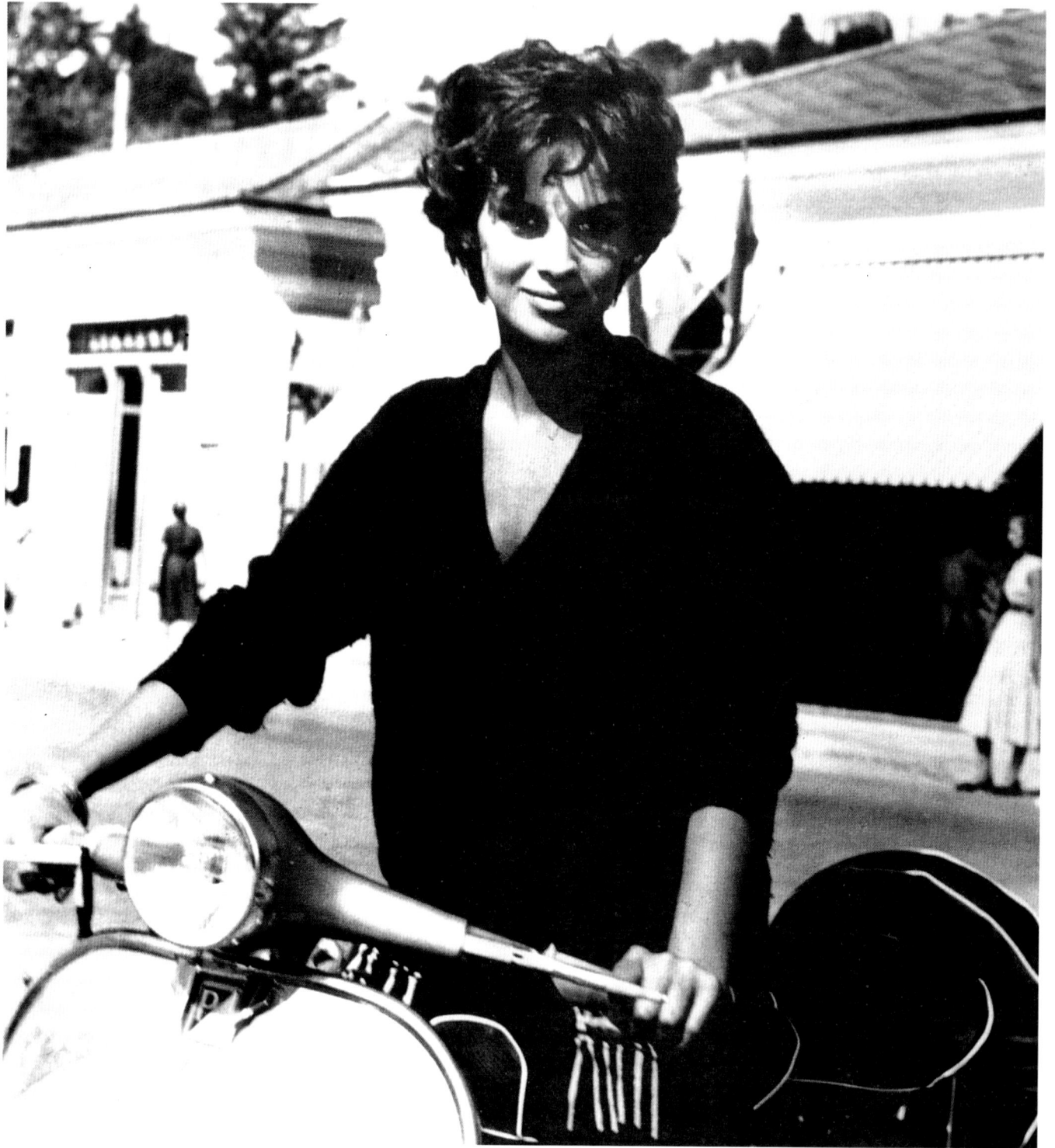

ma, ferocity and violence, characteristics close to high cylinder motorbikes, have never had anything to do with the smiling world of the **Vespa**. This has not limited its dramatic possibilities, though. The **Vespa** has had parts in great films with powerful social messages. Think of *Rocco e i suoi fratelli*, *L'Avventura*, *Mery per sempre*, *Accattone*, *Il Branco*, films of high dramatic content and she quietly played her part with her weight of reality. But the true reign over which she dominated remains the play "il lato assolato della strada". In some way **Vespa** recalls this merriness of living. And with a certain Italian living style, sunny and smiling.

Vacanze Romane, unforgettable film was the first we remembered, but after that, in the same years *Poveri ma belli*, *Bellezze in bicicletta*, *La notte brava*, *Matrimonio all'italiana*, *Le ragazze di Piazza di Spagna*, *Peccato che sia una canaglia*, *Un amore a Roma*, *La bella di Lodi* and so on, all the lovely girls of the cinema screen, one after another, have sat upon that beautiful steel armchair and on its little curves have they flown. In *Mimì metallurgico*, Mimì's Sicilian wife is emancipated when she begins to work in a factory, the symbol of her emancipation was her riding a **Vespa**, after decorously keeping her skirt closed with a safety pin.

As well as for years making us smile along with the most popular, enjoyable and successful films, the **Vespa** has us winking at magazine and newspaper pages. There was no famous personage of the stage, the screen, politics or jet society who didn't finish up plonked upon those curves, content to be photographed for youthful, sportive or fun contexts.

First of all naturally Mister "Volare" (flyer), from the photo, holds onto the **Vespa** with two legs spread right out sideways in the air like a naughty boy, and with one of his loveable acute high notes renders him adorable; Lucia Bosé and Louis Dominguin, both young and gorgeous, she, "Miss Italia" and cinema star, he, illustrious matador, little more than a boy, celebrate their wedding on the terrace of Trinità dei Monti. And from his position and Lucia at his back, the **Vespa** reveals her true nature as an Andalusian pure-bred, like those, which during "il Rosio" of the Siviglian fieras, show off "le muchache" carried on the backs of their horses by their "caballeros". John Wayne, on the other hand, poses on her with a distracted, witty, calm Irish air and it looks as if any minute now he will raise his cap and toast his friends with a lovely cold beer. The adored Gary Cooper with his long legs and heavenly eyes illunmines a spring Rome, sitting with his very long and elegant extremities, on that small she-devil of a friendly motor. Hery Fonda gives us an affectionate smack at poverty, with his cool gait of the west, who standing by our **Vespa**, poses in a Homburg and an English gentleman's coat - the truth is he buys clothes from Italian tailors - the only one in a slovenly sporty appearance is Anthony Perkins, top shirt button undone and even, with exception, smiling.

But the list of film stars is unending, in those years: Poggio, Broderick, Crawford, Masina, Sernas, Interlenghi, and then the descent of Roman stars of fashion in the sixties, la creme de la creme, leaned upon that lucky saddle of the **Vespa**. James Stewart, Judy Holliday, Marina Vlady, Melina Mercury, Tyron Power and Linda Christian. Then she, the **Vespa**, flew in an aeroplane, like all film stars, to go to Park Avenue and exhibit herself where other rotund celebrities had the honour of sitting upon her: Kim Novak, Jane Russell, Marlon Brando, Abbe Lane.

It is not always graceful to name-drop, but one knows, cinema is myth and the names of

Antonella Lualdi in a take from the film *Delitto in fuga*. Following pages: Maurizio Arena and Carlo Sorrentino in *Il simpatico mascalzone*

gods are part of their religion and ceremonies. On the other hand, I don't know if it's got anything to do with the skill of Piaggio's public relations office or simply an irresistable fascination for our star **Vespa**, but the list of "Vespa-rised" names is so glamourous that it is impossible to resist the temptation to continue along down it. They are the most prestigious names of the international Olympus of cinema. From Charlie Chaplin to Gene Kelly, from Rock Hudson to Natalie Wood, Lex Barker. The Italians all ended up possessing her. Elsa Marinelli, Renato Rascel, Anna Maria Ferrero, Sofia Loren, when she still had the "ph" in her name. Giovanna Ralli, Marina Vlady, Alberto Sordi, Vittorio Gasmann. And more: Heflin, Jimmy Durante, Raf Vallone, Renato Salvatori, Richard Conte, Laurent Terzieff. Everyone right up to the super elegant Cary Grant. A success without precedent, galloping upon celluloid wings of a great period of Italian cinema reaching a notoreity on a par with spaghetti.

No one managed to avoid the contagion of the fashion of those times. Not even kings, queens and heads of state. It was when I saw the Pope, the austere and well remembered Montini, caressing her (let's say it) mischievious curves, of that seductive mo-ped, squatting down beside his papal white slippers, under the highest benedication it was that I understood that that was that. The **Vespa** was "raised" to a symbol "urbi et orbi". Another singular fact came afterwards with the passing of time. The fifties and sixties were such vital and particular years with the explosion of the economic boom, that its symbolic signs were very characteristic. And like all signs of a marked character after they strongly signalled an epoch or a period they inevitably tend to remain attached to that period and so pass out of fashion with the passing of time. On leaving fashion, at the most, they enter into history, that is into the glamourous gallery of our past.

But the **Vespa** - in Rome we would say "impunita" (unpunished) didn't at all follow the fate of Lollo, of the purgative Gazzoni, or of the little bird from the radio (translator's note: this bird signified the commencement of radio programs). No our imperturbable star, continued her familiarly triumphant march, while against her an unimaginable bombardment of motorettes, mo-peds, large motorbikes opened up, and a whole infinite number of bands of thundering, rip-roaring two wheeled vehicles which, to maintain being a predilection for the young, filled up the last part of the century with studded leather, leather boots, jackets, belts; chains, helmets and head pieces. Messages, a little pathetic, of violence and machismo of which Brando gave the first consecration with *Il Selvaggio*.

For many centuries vitalism, energy, competition, aggression of the young were channelled and exploited by contemptible men in power, inserting boys into armies and sending them with the sound of marches, hymns, gossip and confused lies, to kill other young people, equally ignorant and prisoners of the same customs and traditions as themselves; saying "it would be cowardice if I don't leave too...". And the confused ideals of the massacre made them vaguely think of their mothers and children, while enveloped in the folds of their country's flag.

Now-a-days that same youthful vitality and energy attracts publicity towards these symbolic objects which tend to give a ferocious and virile image with roaring sounds of motorbikes, behind which the massive army of boys line themselves up in defense of their own weakness and fragility. Of course, much better an army of motorbikers, uncivil, loud violent bands. Always better than armies of victim-assassins of the war or of guerillas, brigades or terrorists. Therefore rather than nothing, better rather.

Opposite:
Urlatori
alla sbarra
in the streets
of Rome.
Joe Sentieri
can be
recognised in
the foreground.
Above:
Marlon Brando,
the Wild One,
trics out
the Vespa

And this: "What is that Kawasaki doing on the beach? It's waiting for the Honda" ("onda" means wave in Italian). We have eaten and digested it even if we can feel a little left in our stomachs.

But... but... as soon as the noisy and smelly wave of the martian motorbike passed by, out from the corner popped her, rounder and friendlier than before. She, the **Vespa**, who has never wanted to associate herself with terroristic aspects: "Facite 'a faccia feroce" (Mime a ferocious face). She, who conserved her agile and care-free charcacter, her affectionate availability typical of things real.

It is extraordinary, the **Vespa**, having been involved in so much fashion, has never passed out of fashion. Times are so advanced, like a large river, and she has remained calm and reassured along the roads of the world. And God knows if along our roads and on our TVs galaxies of vehicles of all kinds will pursue one another and alternate for our pleasure, to make us choose, to make us buy.

She, doesn't seem to need it, incredible, if this hypothesis were true, she would be the first product to navigate tempests and floodings of eras, of fashions and advertisements while keeping afloat without swimming. She is always there, nice instead of nasty, "simpatica" instead of hateful, affectionate instead of violent, and here she still is.

Near the end of the second millenium, again main character in a film. Stupifying. Even more beautiful and unconstrained than before. Leave behind all the "savages", blouson noire, metal, punk and even the rampant motoretta for stealing, which had its moments of glory thanks to "Michelino o Pazzo".

Just yesterday the noble and intellectual buttocks of Moretti gave homage with the new "levers" of cinema to our diva, making her the absolute portagonist of the ironic wanderings of the author, helmet on head and certainty in the heart, which upon her he rode around another Rome. New suburbs, by now bourgeoisie, and new forms. Of course there is no merriment and you would go nuts for want of optimism. But her friendliness and her availability seem to point her out as an ideal means of transport, even today and even for a mental journey of reflexion and verification, upon the pages of an "intellectual diary".

She is always ready for a new adventure and the cinema, I believe, will have her continue soon with new proposals. When Wolkswagen wanted to celebrate itself and financed an American film to launch the "wagon" for the people in the U.S.A. - (perhaps to make them forget the name's Hitlerian roots, they rebaptized it "Beetle") - they attentively observed **Vespas'** history and decided that nice insects are more popular than wagons. The Beetle was successful, but nothing to compare with the eternal youth of the **Vespa**.

Maybe it will be a love story for some Samurai beast who will lose his head for the fresh and clear curves of this "signora" who smiles to him along the Italian roads. Who knows, behind her also the violent and ferocious Samurai will end up by taking off his jacket and chains and will stop to eat a tomato pizza on a meadow in front of the sea.

**Opposite:
Jean-Claude
Brialy
and Laurent
Terzieff,
in Rome, during
the shooting
of the film
La notte brava,
directed
by Mauro
Bolognini**

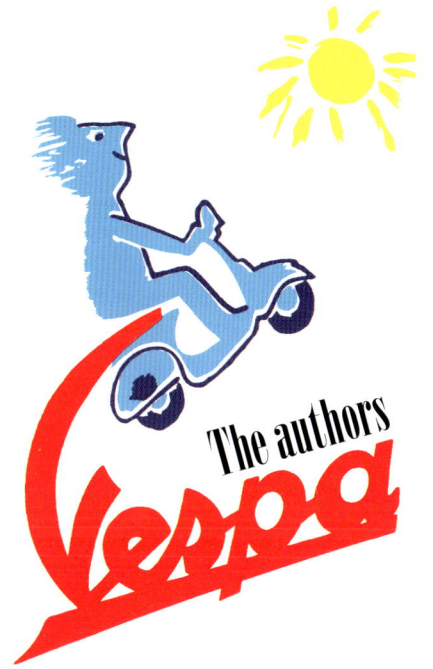

The authors

Umberto Eco

Umberto Eco was born in Alessandria on January 1, 1932. After graduating in Philosophy (Turin, 1954), he was appointed university professor of Aesthetics (1961), and since 1975 has been full professor of Semiotics at the University of Bologna, where he is the President of the degree course in Communication Sciences. He is director of the magazine "VS-Quaderni di Studi Semiotici". He has taught in many foreign universities (Harvard, Yale, Columbia, Collège de France, École Normale Superieure) and is a Honorary Fellow of Kellog College, Oxford. He has also received 19 degrees "honoris causa". Among his major scientific and literary works are: *Il problema estetico in San Tommaso,* 1956; *Opera aperta,* (1962); *La ricerca della lingua perfetta,* (1993); *Sei passeggiate nei boschi narrativi,* (1994); *Il nome della rosa,* (1980); *Il pendolo di Foucault,* (1988); *L'isola del giorno prima,* (1992). His works have been translated in thirty-two languages. He is contributor to several Italian and foreign newspapers and magazines, and is presently editor of a weekly column for the magazine "L'Espresso".

Omar Calabrese

Omar Calabrese is full professor of Mass Communication in the course of Communication Sciences at the University of Siena and of Sociology of Culture in the course of Public Relations at IULM Institute in Milan. The author of many essays on Mass Communication (*L'età neobarocca,* 1987, *Mille di questi anni,* 1990, and with Ugo Volli *I telegiornali,* 1995), he also edited with Maurizio Boldrini the book *Il libro della Comunicazione,* published by Piaggio in 1995. In 1995 Calabrese was appointed "Assessore alla Cultura" (Councillor for Culture) by the town council of Siena.

Maurizio Bettini

Maurizio Bettini, born in 1947, is full professor of Classical Philology at the "Facoltà di Lettere e Filosofia" (Department of Humanities) of Siena University, where he was appointed dean from 1986 to 1995. He is presently director of the Center for Anthropological Interdisciplinary Studies on Ancient Culture at the University of Siena. He has taught at the universities of Pisa, Venice, at Johns Hopkins University in Baltimore and is at present visiting professor at the Department of Classics of Berkeley University, California. The founder and general secretary of the association for interdisciplinary studies "Antropologia e mondo antico" in Siena, his research is mainly oriented towards the anthropology of the ancient world. He is also a frequent contributor to the cultural pages of the Italian newspaper "La Repubblica". Among his major publications are *Antropologia e cultura Romana,* La Nuova Italia Scientifica, Rome 1986; *Il ritratto dell'amante,* Einaudi, Turin 1992; *Lo straniero, ovvero l'identità culturale a confronto* (editor), Laterza, Bari 1992; *I classici nell'età dell'indiscrezione,* Einaudi, Torino 1994.

Tommaso Fanfani

Tommaso Fanfani was born at Pieve Santo Stefano, near Arezzo, in 1943. He has been full professor of Philosophy at the Department of Economic History of the University of Pisa since 1980. The author of more than 90 publications, his research is mainly focused on the history of Eighteenth Century economical thought and modern and contemporary economic History, as attested by his many monographs on these subjects. He recently shifted his attention to the Nineteenth and Twentieth Centuries, orienting his studies towards Business History (*The Troublesome Development of a Protected Industry: Italian Shipping from 1861 to 1914,* 1983) and the general economic development of Italy in the late post-war period (*Scelte politiche e fatti economici nel quarantennio repubblicano,* 1986). A member of distinguished scientific committees of Italian and foreign specialised magazines, he has held several academic posts at the Athenaeum of Pisa, where he was recently appointed dean of the "Facoltà di Economia e Commercio" (Faculty of Business and Economics).

François Burkhardt

François Burkhardt was born in Winterthur, Switzerland, in 1936. After completing his studies in Architecture at ETH in Losanne and at HfBK in Hamburg, he worked with some of the most important architectural companies, including the *Urban Design Group* of Berlin and Hamburg. His co-operation with international cultural institutions culminated in the role of director (from 1984 to 1990) of the *Centre de Créations Industriel* at the *Centre George Pompidou* in Paris. Burkhardt, who taught History and Theory of Design at the Schools of Art in Vienna and Saarbrücken, has organised 150 exhibitions all over the world and is the author of many publications regarding Arts, Architecture and Design. Advisor to the board of public institutions and private companies in Germany, France, Belgium, Austria and Italy, Burkhardt is presently director of the Architecture magazine *Domus*.

Francesca Picchi

Francesca Picchi was born in Milan in 1963 and graduated in Architecture at the Milan Polytechnic. She has been a contributor to the architecture and design magazine Domus since 1994.

Sebastiano Vassalli

Sebastiano Vassalli was born in Genoa, Italy, and presently lives in Piedmont, where he has spent many years of his life. In his youth he was a member of the "gruppo 63" and took part in the "experimentalism" artistic trend. His more recent fiction novels, which have all been published in Italy by Einaudi, are: *La notte della cometa* (1984), *L'oro del mondo* (1987), *La chimera* (1990), *Marco e Mattio* (1992), *Il cigno* (1994) and *3012* (1995). He used to write for the Italian newspaper "La Repubblica" and is at present a contributor to the newspaper "Il Corriere della Sera".

Francesco Alberoni

After early research into emotional and cognitive processes, Alberoni shifted to sociology, studying the star-system and the consumer (*Consumi e società*, 1964). He made a fundamental contribution to the study of collective movements with the concept of dawning civilization (*Movimento e istituzione*, 1977); and then applied these concepts to the process of falling in love in the book *Innamoramento e amore* (1979), which brought him international renown. He has also studied friendship, eroticism, envy and moral experiences. Among his summary work are *Genesi* (1989), on movements, and *Ti amo* (1996), on love. He is presently full professor at the IULM University in Milan.

Marino Livolsi

Marino Livolsi (Milan, 1937) is full professor of "Sociologia della Comunicazione" (Sociology of Communication) and director of the "Istituto di Comunicazione" (Communication Institute) at IULM University in Milan. Previously, he has also held the post of faculty dean at the University of Trento and of Vice President of the Communication Knowledge and Culture of the International Sociological Association. His research is focused on mass-media communication and culture, with specific attention to child socialisation, sub-cultures and consumer. Among his many essays, Identità e progetto and L'Italia che cambia. He recently wrote the book La realtà virtuale. La TV in Italia negli anni '90, on Italian TV in the nineties.

Gilberto Filippetti

Gilberto Filippetti, born in the town of Jesi in the "Marche" region of Italy, led for many years the creative office of the Florentine advertising agency "Leader". He has created some of the most powerful and provocative advertising campaigns of the last twenty-five years including, together with those conceived for Piaggio ("Chi Vespa...", "Sardomobili", "Gente solare", to mention only the ones that are immediately recognisable for the Italian public), "Verde la vita" for the Sasso brand of olive oil, "Sào è suo" for a coffee brand, and "Chi ama brucia", the well-remembered ad for the "Pavesini" biscuits. Filippetti, who now considers himself a "true" Florentine, lives and works in the Tuscan regional capital.

Alessandro Baricco

Alessandro Baricco, a writer and musical reviewer, was born in Turin in 1958. He is the author of 3 fiction novels, *Castelli di rabbia* (Rizzoli 1991 and Bompiani 1994), *Oceano mare* (Rizzoli 1993), *Seta* (Rizzoli 1996), *Novecento* (Feltrinelli 1994) a novel/monologue on which a theatre play has recently been based, and two musical review essays, *Il genio in fuga* (Il Melangolo 1988, in print, Einaudi) and *L'anima di Hegel e le mucche del Wisconsin* (Garzanti 1992). In 1996 he completed the theatre script *Davila Roa,* specially written for the director Luca Ronconi. He is also a contributor to the newspaper "La Repubblica" and a teacher at the Holden School for writing technique, founded by himself and a group of friends in 1994.

Antonio Tabucchi

Antonio Tabucchi, born in Pisa in 1943, is full professor of Portuguese Literature at the University of Siena. Among his fiction publications, that have been translated into many languages and appreciated all over the world, we may mention *Piazza d'Italia* (1975), *Il gioco del rovescio* (1981), *Piccoli equivoci senza importanza* (1985), *Il filo dell'orizzonte* (1986), *Requiem* (1992) and the recent best-seller *Sostiene Pereira*, on which the movie of the same name with Marcello Mastroianni was based. Among the literary awards won by Tabucchi are "Médicis Etranger", "Viareggio", "Campiello" and the European Award "Jean Monnet". Tabucchi has also translated the work of Fernando Pessoa into Italian.

Lina Wertmuller

Lina Wertmuller, a renowned Italian theatre and cinema director, was born in Rome in the characteristic neighbourhood of "quartiere Prati", where she still lives with her husband Enrico Job, an art director and scenery designer. After her early training at Pietro Sharoff's (a pupil of the great Stanislawsky) School of Theatre, in 1951 she founded, together with some Academy fellows, the avant-garde theatre of Santo Stefano in Cacco, in Rome. Her success as a theatre director began with the staging of her play *Amore e magia nella cucina di Mamma* ("Love and magic in Mom's kitchen") and has recently been consecrated, among other productions, by the direction of Bizet's *Carmen* at the San Carlo theatre in Naples. Her first experience in the world of cinema was with Federico Fellini, who chose her as his assistant director for the movie *8 e 1/2*. Her first movie, *I basilischi*, won the second prize at the Locarno Film Festival and started a brilliant career, spangled by many movies: *Mimì metallurgico...*, *Travolti da un insolito destino...*, *Pasqualino settebellezze* (four Oscar nominations) and her recent *Ninfa plebea*. In 1988 Lina Wertmuller was appointed Special Commissioner of the Roman "Centro Sperimentale di Cinematografia".

Printed in Italy
by Alpigraf
Industria Grafica
Maggio 2001